Through The Eyes Of An Addict

Patrick Sean Naish

Copyright © 2024 Ralph Naish.

All rights reserved. No part of this book may be reproduced, stored, or transmitted by any means—whether auditory, graphic, mechanical, or electronic—without written permission of both publisher and author, except in the case of brief excerpts used in critical articles and reviews. Unauthorized reproduction of any part of this work is illegal and is punishable by law.

ISBN: 979-8-89419-509-4 (sc)
ISBN: 979-8-89419-510-0 (hc)
ISBN: 979-8-89419-511-7 (e)

Because of the dynamic nature of the Internet, any web addresses or links contained in this book may have changed since publication and may no longer be valid. The views expressed in this work are solely those of the author and do not necessarily reflect the views of the publisher, and the publisher hereby disclaims any responsibility for them.

One Galleria Blvd., Suite 1900, Metairie, LA 70001
(504) 702-6708

CONTENTS

Prologue vii
Introduction xi
Chapter 1:   Behind the eyes of an addict 1
Chapter 2:   Birth of an addict 6
Chapter 3:   Adrenalin Becomes A Drug 11
Chapter 4:   "A Wake Up Call" 16
Chapter 5:   "Fatal Coolness" 23
Chapter 6:   "Behind Bars" 29
Chapter 7:   "California Dreaming" 37
Chapter 8:   "California Nightmare" 46
Chapter 9:   "California Ash" 54
Chapter 10: "The Walking Dead: An Introspective" 63
Chapter 11: "Defenseless" 71
Chapter 12: "Responsibility Comes Second" 78
Chapter 13: "A New Master" 85
Chapter 14: "The Intervention" 93
Chapter 15: "Insanity Takes Hold" 102
Chapter 16: "Chaos Ensues" 110
Chapter 17: "Missed Opportunities" 119
Chapter 18: "A Moment Of Clarity" 128
Chapter 19: "Rehab" 135
Chapter 20: "Bottom At Last" 143
Chapter 21: "Testing Sobriety" 151
Chapter 22: "A New Tomorrow" 162
Chapter 23: "Closure" 172
Epilogue 1 179
Epilogue 2 183

- Poems from the Heart of an Addict ... 187
  - A Conversation With God ... 188
  - A Daydream ... 190
  - A Hard Pattern To Break ... 192
  - A New Road ... 194
  - A Time For Black Thoughts ... 196
  - An Escape From The Flames ... 198
  - Assimilation ... 200
  - Dreams Revisited ... 202
  - Echoes Of A Childs Laughter ... 204
  - From Black To Light ... 206
  - Guilt ... 208
  - I'm Sad, I'm Angry ... 210
  - I Have ... 213
  - Like The Wolf ... 215
  - Lost Miracle ... 216
  - Misconceptions ... 219
  - My Friend ... 220
  - My Process ... 222
  - One Last Hit ... 224
  - Purgatory ... 226
  - Rebirth ... 229
  - Repayment ... 231
  - Shall We Dream ... 233
  - Something Deeper ... 235
  - Stop! ... 237
  - Take Heed Addiction ... 239
  - Thank You ... 242
  - The Hunt ... 244
  - The Judgment ... 247
  - Together ... 249
  - Two Directions ... 251
  - Who Am I? ... 254
  - Yesterday And Today ... 256
- About the Author ... 259

I first read "Through the Eyes of an Addict" chapter by chapter as it was being written, shortly after deciding to make Sean my friend as he began his Recovery journey. Re-reading it now, 12 years later, the book now final and complete with the thoughtful and touching prologue, epilogues, and sadly a eulogy by his family, simultaneously saddens and inspires me as to what is possible in the wake of the deceit, destruction, depravity, and misery that the disease of Addiction wreaks through its victims. You may prefer accomplice to, rather than victim of, the disease however the results are horrific all the same. Sean's addiction experience is indeed horrific; and his book a thrilling, dark, and frightening tale (if you can forget that it is not fiction) that illuminates clearly the mind of a using addict. The contradictions swirl inclusive of insanity and lucidity, pride and humility, selfishness and compassion, shame and callousness, and finally wanting to be clean and sober as well as wanting nothing more than to use and die. In reading you will, as I did, surely notice how Sean did eventually become fully aware that he could recover despite the carnage, and availed himself often of the daily reprieve a program of recovery offers during the final twelve years of his life to good effect. If you don't read to the end, you might never believe that he became a good friend, father, son, brother, and compassionate helper to countless lost souls in his Recovery. About the book, I am reminded of the humility, intellect, wit, and incredible insight into himself that Sean demonstrates and lived as a recovering addict. He could easily have been materially wealthy in his recovery, however chose to dedicate his life to helping others in a profession that paid not well, and being the best father he could be. His book ought to be a resource to addicts in the grip, addicts seeking Recovery, and in particular to those close to an addict as it demonstrates the insanity of an addict both wanting to be good, yet repeating the same mistakes. It shows how one can intellectually understand the "why" and "how" one gets caught up in Addiction, the depths one can sink, yet still be unable to stop without help. Recovery is possible, wherever one's "bottom" may lie, as Sean's life demonstrates, and detailed in the final chapters as he relates his first year of sobriety. Make no mistake, Sean did relapse from time to time, however his Recovery as evidenced by the relationships with his son, his other family, his friends, his co-workers, and his clients, in my view, count large as weighed against the resulting anguish borne by himself and those who knew and loved him during a relapse. I am reminded, re-reading his book, also of his friendship, which was unconditional. Recovery is not a war to be won, it is a series of battles with yourself that can be won with the help and support of loving and caring resources. His legacy, with this book, will be to pass along his experience, strength, and hope.

Dave Rassell

PROLOGUE

The following is the autobiographical account of the life of a young man beset by the insidious disease that we know as addiction. One of the most prominent symptoms of this disease is that addicts are very adept at donning a mask. It is the addict's intention that no one see behind the mask. This makes it extremely difficult for those of us who are trying, from the outside, to understand and to help the victims of this disease.

To have someone who is an addict, highly intelligent and articulate, voluntarily rip away his mask and bear his soul as Sean has done in this book is rare indeed. Sean's motive in doing this was threefold. First, Sean spent most of his working career trying to "give back" or help others suffering from this disease and he thought that this book might be another avenue of help. Secondly, Sean though that this book would help people like his close family members understand, deal with and help an addict. Thirdly, Sean was trying to understand himself.

I don't believe that anyone can read this book without grasping the unrelenting pain, torture, and self-abasement of the "user" caused by the disease of addiction; nor do I believe that one can fail to grasp the pain and suffering inflicted upon the "user's" friends and family.

Yes, addiction is a disease, and like any other disease we seek "medication" for it. Unfortunately the medication sought by an addict only feeds the disease. Unlike the medication a doctor prescribes, the medication from a dealer may be laced with anything including other potentially deadly drugs forcing the addict to play Russian roulette with every hit. Far, far too many pull the trigger on the loaded cylinder!

If you are an addict, I must ask you, is your "high", or as is often the case after becoming addicted, not even a "high" so much as just a temporary relief from the pain of your addiction or trauma, really worth inflicting *this* upon yourself and upon those who love you? There are people, programs and institutions, detox centers, rehabs, recovery houses, counselors and God himself waiting to help you off this treadmill. However, none of them can help without your willingness to be helped; without you having the will and the courage to seek them out. *For the sake of those who love you, for your sake, for Sean's sake I beg you, seek them out now!*

R.P. Naish

This book is dedicated to many.

To God, without whose strength true recovery is impossible.

To my family and friends who, although they traversed the hell I put them through, were there for me with their love, even if sometimes they had no choice but to demonstrate that love by kicking me out of their lives until I took the first step.

Mostly this book is dedicated to my son who simply by being saved my life and my soul. Zachary you are my inspiration and my hope for a better tomorrow.

INTRODUCTION

Take my hand as I lead you through my story.

There will be times on this journey that you will surely hate me. There will be times when my self-hatred is recognizable. More often than not there will be times that regardless of the relationship we forge as we progress, I will need your shoulder to lean on. I will need you to dry my tears.

My motives for writing this are not entirely altruistic. For a man who has had a lifetime of internalizing his emotions, pushing everyone away and hiding behind a self-created wall, the prospect of pouring my soul out to all those who read this is terrifying beyond measure.

It is in evaluation of this fear that I realize this is the path to start healing. As such I can't claim that this endeavor is for those I encounter but rather is a self-serving attempt at emptying my soul of the pain I carry, the shame I hide and the guilt I visit upon others in the form of hostility.

There is also the hope that regardless of how poorly this may turn out perhaps one who has suffered as those of us with this disease have will read it and know that there is help available. It has taken over 17 years of drug abuse, a lifetime of wasted years, continuous scrapes with death and the help of many others to realize that at the end of the day we are only as alone as we chose to be or allow our disease to keep us.

I hope to attack the common perceptions of those who suffer from addiction; I hope to make people think. If, at the end, you think I am wrong then at least you considered addiction long enough to come to this conclusion. I made you, the reader, contemplate what you have read and that accomplishes at least one of my goals.

I pledge to be as honest with you as my soul allows, regardless of the depths of depravity or the vulnerability I will feel. Those who read this will learn of things that I have never told anyone before. They will have insight into my being and to one such as me who has made a life out of showing to others no more than the bare minimum this is fear incarnate.

So grab your tissues, I'll need them and perhaps so will you. Take courage as we both may need to rely on it and come with me. I offer no pledges of a happy ending. This I can never promise anyone, not even myself, but I do swear to you that until the day I stop writing either from death or fear I will keep trying to be there the next day, clean and sober, so that we may continue our journey.

> "I've seen the needle and the damage done, a little part of it in everyone, but every junkie is like a setting Sun."
>
> The Needle And The Damage Done
> Neil Young

Chapter 1

Behind the eyes of an addict

How are you my Friend? I am honored that you have decided to take this journey with me. It is my plan to exorcize some demons, to shine light on those things I keep hidden deep within myself. My life has been an exercise in hiding from emotions and it is beyond time that I face these buried skeletons.

I have heard that emotional development stops or at the very least is significantly slowed when one starts abusing alcohol or drugs. If this is accurate then this negative effect started for me at about the age of 13. Given the physical effects drug abuse has on my body I feel like I am 90. I am one of the few that while laughing at a low brow humor fart joke would be pulling their pants up to their arm pits and bitching about the government. This said I shall try and face the emotional pitfalls I envision with courage.

Before we begin there are a few things I want to state:

Firstly I know that my experiences in addiction and in life are not unique nor are they as bad as the path I know others have had to follow. Through the examination of my personal journey it is my hope that I will remove some of the power from those contributing factors that push me towards self-destruction.

Secondly I offer no cures. Addiction is a disease that although it cannot be removed can be kept in remission. Although I don't pretend to know all the answers I do believe I know where they can be found. We shall discuss that later.

What better place to start our trek than behind the eyes, or in my head. To examine the thoughts and attitudes that have played such an intrinsic part in both my development and my day to day activities. I believe that our actions and thoughts are a constant precursor to our futures. Buried negative emotions such as guilt and shame that fester like cancer in our subconscious only serve to poison our efforts to strive towards a better tomorrow.

So let us start by examining those emotional attitudes that I have carried for so long. Step inside my head, since I have been told I have a lot of space between my ears, feel free to stretch out and let us begin. Imagine you are alone on a beach. The sand provides a perfect resting place as you lie back and enjoy the warm caress of the sun. The waves, gently breaking on the shore sound more like a lullaby than anything else and soon you are transported to an almost utopian state. Now imagine that regardless of this perfection there is an overwhelming sensation of unworthiness. It is almost as if the beach itself finds your presence repugnant. Everyone may come and enjoy this serenity but you.

This is a demonstration of the lack of self-worth that has plagued me since I can remember. It seems that every personal interaction has been tainted by the deep seated thought that I do not belong. As you will learn later I have had success both in my personal life and in business only to find that in retrospect this lack of confidence has reared its ugly head. Like a destructive alter ego it has ensured that I have taken action to sabotage any happiness I have found.

I have pushed those around me away, convinced that they would only hurt me. When they left, I had been certain that their departure was inevitable given it was only a matter of time before they found out what I was truly about, who I really was. Logically I know, I have a lot to offer yet the inner demons, perhaps the disease of addiction itself, convinced me I am not worthy of people's love.

In life I have found success in business, made good money and earned the respect of my peers for my accomplishments. Once again, however, I have disrupted my life in such a way as to ensure I have removed those things that have brought me success. These actions will become apparent as I later describe some of the more significant events in my life.

It is has long been a misguided belief of mine that any display of sadness is a sign of weakness. Those who displayed such emotions through tears were to be ridiculed or worse taken advantage of. Later as I sunk deeper into the world of drugs, dealers and street life I learned that such demonstrations can even be fatal.

With this belief in mind I have become an expert at stuffing down my emotions, especially those of a depressing nature. I have hidden these sad feelings from everyone. I have even tried, without success, to deny their existence entirely. However for all my efforts I am cognizant of the fact that I am a very empathetic and even sensitive person. I may witness some misfortune befall someone and will probably be so crass as to make a joke at their expense, to laugh at their troubles, but secretly I am internalizing their pain.

For some unknown reason I seem to duplicate what I think they are feeling and immediately I stuff that emotion where it joins a lifetime of such experiences and grows. I have continued to add others pain to my own and have carried this with me for what seems an eternity.

I vividly remember an incident involving an apparently abandoned dog following me home in the rain. I was certain I would not be allowed to keep the animal and so as I neared home I ran ahead of it and closed the door behind me barring its entrance into the house. Later I sat in my bedroom and watched the dog sit out-front in the rain and cold awaiting my return.

This happened when I was less than seven and although at the time I refused to cry I still carry that sadness with me. The pain of that moment seems as fresh as the day it happened and even now as I relay this to you, my friend, I feel a deep fear that it will only serve as a tool for ridicule. That somehow I have gone soft, "associates" in my old circles will find out and they in turn will take advantage of me. In the telling of such a thing I feel weak and vulnerable.

If the story of the dog troubles me so much to tell you than imagine the discomfort I face in the prospect of sharing other more significant events.

Isn't it amazing how significant guilt can be in our lives? There is no doubt that guilt does have its place. How would we know if certain actions are in violation of our morals if we never felt guilt?

Yet guilt has played such an incredibly major part in my life it is hard to imagine functioning without it. I would even go so far as to feel guilty for having emotions in the first place. I will feel happy that perhaps a card game turned out in my favor and then will immediately feel guilty for that happiness. I will be in a situation where I am perfectly entitled to be most concerned with my own wellbeing but immediately feel that I am self-centered.

Such overwhelming and constant guilt only serves as an emotional restraint refusing to allow me to go free and yet I still wonder what right I have to want to rid myself of it. As far as addiction is concerned guilt can kill. It only feeds the cycle that is addiction in the first place. You take an action that causes you to feel guilt, your disease of addiction senses the negative emotions and convinces you that "we don't need to feel this" and so you use drugs. This of course causes more guilt and the circle continues.

In my addiction I have done many things that simply make me cringe when I think about them. The guilt is so strong and at the same time I carry guilt from things I have done over 20 years ago.

One of the most common traits associated with the behavioral standbys of an addict is that of the mask. We hide behind a fictitious persona that allows us to be whoever we feel we need to be in any specific situation. First and foremost the mask allows us to hide our true identity. Once again believing no one wants to know the real person so we pretend to be someone else.

Unfortunately as my addiction grew or as I became more and more lost in that addiction the ability to act as I perceived best suited the situation became a tool for manipulating others.

Even in my professional life my talent in demonstrating traits I thought the other person wanted to see was of benefit as it enabled me to be successful in sales. Later as I used this in my addiction it allowed me to convince others to give me money, feel sorry for me or generally do what I wanted.

A fear of demonstrating my true self eventually turned into a self-destructive habit than enabled my addiction to grow.

I am aware, logically, that I have many attributes, that I have a significant role to play on this Earth and that I have much to offer. Subsequently as we delve deeper into how the negative emotions I carry have affected my life it is my hope that I will be able to dispense with the baggage and allow those positive elements of my person to shine through.

I have always carried a disproportionate amount of anger, stuffing each event that has caused anger deeper until I often lash out in totally counterproductive ways. This anger manifests itself in other less obvious ways, sarcasm, open hostility and of course guilt.

To date I have yet to find a proper outlet for all of these negative emotions that dwell inside of me. I have always turned to drugs to self medicate against the pain, to quiet that which wants to escape. This inability to deal with painful emotions is common among those who abuse drugs.

Even if you're not an addict perhaps my exploration of my inner workings will allow you to relate to some demons you may be carrying, hopefully together you and I will truly learn that "God don't make junk".

Chapter 2

Birth of an addict

Like many of my brethren I was born an addict. However I am sure the very early years of my life are inconsequential to the story I am going to tell you. So let us fast forward through those first years. Past first teeth and first birthdays, skimming past first steps and first knee scrapes.

We will jump directly to my first "hard drug" experience. In retrospect even I am surprised at what an early age this occurred and although I didn't realize it at the time I can now look back on it and recognize that my reaction to the drug was synonymous with addiction.

To properly relate the experience to you I need to inundate you with some background. I have a medical condition called Severe Laryngospasm. This is where the larynx will inadvertently close due to a reflex action. When I was about 8 or 9 years old I had to have Rhinoplasty surgery during which they had to insert a tube down my throat to assist in breathing. Unknown to the Doctor at the time was my Laryngospasm condition; thus when the tube was inserted my larynx went into spasm making it impossible to breath.

Therefore the medical staff decided to do the surgery under a local anesthetic. The medication they gave me for pain and, I suppose, as a sedative, was liquid cocaine. To this day I can vividly remember the drug taking effect and even more significant than the sudden feeling of euphoria was that all my nervousness over the operation vanished. All my insecurities, guilty feelings and concerns disappeared along with it.

At the time I felt as if I had in that moment been reborn, free and clear of the chains that were dragging me down.

Even at the age of 8 I truly believed that I had discovered that for which I had subconsciously been searching my entire life. This was truly a miracle.

Later as the medication wore off I had a very distinct feeling of panic. The returning fears and insecurities were like a black cloud awaiting the disappearance of that which had provided me this brief protection.

Luckily for me, at the time I made no correlation between the drugs and this sense of freedom and internal peace. Even as I delved deeper into my addiction later in life I was still blind to the connection. My next experience wasn't for several years later when, in early junior high school, I was being treated for an ongoing problem with severe migraine headaches. The Doctor had tried everything and finally resorted to two medications to treat the problem. Although I cannot remember the names of either medication I certainly remember the effects.

First thing in the morning I would take a pill that would leave me bouncing off the walls. It was amazing! I would wake tired and groggy and within twenty minutes of taking this pill I was ready to take on the world. Once again the problems that had seemed so heavy the day before were gone and I was left free and clear of any emotional hindrance.

After lunch I would take the second pill and if the first was amazing in how energetic I felt the second was equally significant in how sluggish I was left. Even though the simple act of walking became a huge effort I was also filled with an incredible sense of relaxation and tranquility. Problems I may have been experiencing with other classmates, my family or teachers were suddenly put into perspective and simply didn't matter. They were a concern for another day.

Even though my drug experiences were sporadic at this age I was still exhibiting those behaviors which I have later learned to identify as those that are common among addicts. I was the kid in class who was desperate for attention and equally terrified I would receive it. Always the class clown I did everything I could think of to draw attention to myself and yet when that attention was delivered I somehow resented it. I absorbed it into my subconscious as an act of aggression or ridicule by those that had responded to my attempts to have them notice me.

Furthermore every action I took to draw attention usually left me with an overwhelming sense of guilt. If I acted out in class I would relish the laughter I received then immediately feel bad for the target of my verbal jabs, usually the teacher and the guilt would kick in. Even though I was fully aware of the chances that the specific behavior would result in punishment I was able to convince myself not to be concerned with the consequences.

One such instance of this type of behavior came in grade five. Our math teacher just happened to be the elderly Principal of our Elementary School. As she wrote on the chalkboard I flicked broken bread clips at her. Each time they struck the chalkboard they made a ringing sound resulting in the teacher jumping. No matter how fast she whirled to catch those parties who were guilty of this she didn't catch me. This continued until finally the Principal literally broke down in front of the class. She started laughing, than quickly began crying, immediately followed up by a screaming fit that spun back into hysterical laughter.

To the shock and horror of my fellow students this awful cycle continued for several minutes until finally a teacher from the class next door came in and helped this poor lady out of the room. I later found out she'd had a nervous breakdown in front of us. She never taught again.

I would be lying if I said my intention in telling this story wasn't to alleviate some of the burden of guilt I feel over this incident; but more important than having you the reader struggle through my confession, I relay this to you to demonstrate the lengths that I would go to for attention. Even at the moment though unaware of the personal consequences or the consequences to others, I pushed forward in a specific course of action because at the time I could feel the approving eyes of my classmates on me.

After the second teacher removed my victim from the class room I was repulsed by my actions and found the laughter of my classmates repugnant. It is without exaggeration that I tell you that I feel guilt for that deplorable act to this day.

Even more significant than attention getting measures were my attempts at isolation; often preferring to be alone than in the company of others. My imagination, which had always been active, became my closest companion. Although not aware of it I had serious problems with trust. For some reason I have been unable to pinpoint, I have always had an extremely difficult time in trusting anyone around me, always convinced that at some point they would betray me. My choices therefore were simply to either hurt them first or remove myself both physically and emotionally from any interpersonal relationships.

I had learned at an early age that if I built that emotional wall high and thick enough no one could get in and if no one could get in they couldn't hurt me. Many times through my childhood I would develop a strong friendship with someone only to find a way to sabotage it.

Growing up I had one best friend. We were close for many, many years until one night during a soccer game we got into a physical fight. Even now as I look back on it I am shocked by my intensity during the altercation. After several moments of exchanging blows with my friend I gained, momentarily, the upper hand and proceeded to launch myself on him as he lay prone throwing punches and kicks with an animalistic ferocity until finally I was dragged off of him.

I remember that after I collected myself the sense of betrayal I felt was overwhelming. The internal pain I was experiencing was beyond anything I had ever been through before. Even though my culpability for the event was equal to his, somehow I felt as if the wrong should all be attributed to him. After that we never really spoke again. I often wonder what became of him and if he feels the same sensation of missed opportunities for kinship that I do. Even now I feel a sense of loss, lost bike rides, lost sporting events; lost double dates…..lost friendship.

I know that everyone has difficult experiences in their childhood so I do not feel unique. Like so many other addicts though I do believe that since we are unable to deal with these emotional dilemmas we carry the scars of these issues with us for the rest of our lives or until we learn to deal with them in a constructive manner.

Without the understanding or ability to process these harmful memories is it any wonder so many of us turn to any substance or action that brings us relief?

Chapter 3

Adrenalin Becomes A Drug

Long before I delved into the world of drugs I found a temporary solution to my need for a rush. This was satisfied through adrenalin. I didn't go bungee jumping or cliff diving. I found all the excitement I needed in acting out in class, fighting authority and criminal activity.

Unfortunately I believe that this desire to explore the darker side of my nature was a significant factor when I did start to live in the drug world for even now I know that part of my addiction was to the danger and excitement I found in the realm of drug deals, avoiding the police and other illegal activity.

My first real foray into anything criminal was at the age of approximately 14. It happened as follows:

I was staying over for the night at a friend's house, given that his house was the easiest to sneak out of without waking his parents. After escaping we spent some time patrolling the alleys around the neighborhood checking car doors. I don't believe we had any intention of stealing a car it was simply the rush of going into someone else's property wondering if at any moment the owner would burst from their house, or perhaps a passing police cruiser might happen by. However we were 14 and were invincible.

After having successfully gained entry into several cars, taking loose change, music cassettes and any other small items lying around we stumbled across an older car in poor condition. Finding the doors unlocked we commenced, as normal, to raid the vehicle for anything we felt was of value.

My friend, who was in the driver seat at the time, and I scoured the vehicle until I happened to check the glove compartment where I came upon car keys. Without thinking I reached over and stuck them into the ignition. They fit perfectly and when I turned them the car fired up. With great shock and fear in his eyes my friend stared at me "What are you doing? Where the hell did you get those?" he exclaimed. I too was equally as fearful of what had just happened and immediately turned the car off.

Without saying anything further both of us jumped from the car and ran to the other side of the apartment building from where we had found this vehicle. We were both out of breath and scared out of our minds but neither one, of course, wanted to admit this for fear of looking weak so we both broke out into nervous laughter.

Almost at once the verbal jousting and dares began. Both of us boasting how if it were up to us we would easily take the car but knowing how chicken the other was we should just walk away. That is how we found ourselves returning to the vehicle, reclaiming it and driving off. Two 14 year olds had just committed their first felony.

I must admit even now as I think back on that experience I can taste the adrenalin in the back of my throat and feel the fast beating of my heart. I experience again the sense of liberation that, if even only for that short term, my actions had freed me from every other issue in my life that seemed now so common place and so inconsequential when compare to fleeing the scene of your first crime.

We cruised around in the stolen property for several hours. Although we were cognizant of the fact we had committed this crime and should be wary of police, we still believed that we were two who couldn't be found out; that somehow we were above the normal processes that occur when someone is caught.

To my shame however the adrenalin that we experienced when we first stole the car died down, and I look back on my next actions as very indicative of the disease of addiction. As soon as the initial rush started to fade I immediately starting concentrating on something to replace it. We drove dangerously for a while to find that feeling again and in truth given the maneuvers we took we are both lucky to be alive today.

Regardless of the fact we were driving well beyond our ability, endangering ourselves and whoever was unfortunate enough to be out at that time of the morning, once again the rush faded and had to be replaced. This is where we got the brilliant idea to take the vehicle to an underground parking lot where we could take turns smashing into the cement walls and support columns.

Finally common sense started to kick in and perhaps even guilt and we both decided to return the car to where we had found it. We drove back with the sun just starting its rise for the day. Both of us tired and yet somehow under the impression that through our activities we had moved one step closer to manhood.

Without being detected we dropped off the vehicle and made good our escape. Where this story takes a nasty turn for me is that, without my knowing it at the time my friend returned to the car the next evening. Apparently the owner hadn't inspected the car, and my friend took it again. The following day my friend called and said he would pick me up after school. In spite of a feeling of doom starting to rise in my belly I agreed.

The next day came and I stood waiting for an hour for his arrival. Instinctively I knew something was wrong and decided to go home. I honestly wasn't surprised when later that evening the phone rang and the caller identified himself as a Constable with the local police. Apparently my friend and another had been arrested for theft. Somehow they had driven the car into an area where it got stuck and had fled. Unfortunately one of my friends had left his wallet in the car and they both returned to retrieve the forgotten property and found the police waiting for them. I can honestly say that at the time I didn't exactly hang out with what you would call future NASA candidates.

It turns out it didn't take much prying for the police to learn of my involvement. To be truthful, it was several years before I got over the sensation of having been ratted out and of realizing that the police had been dealing with two very scared fourteen year olds, thus making their job very easy.

What stands out for me through that whole incident, beyond the satisfaction I found in the adrenalin, is the look on my Mothers face when the officer told her I would have to report to the police station where I would be placed under arrest and questioned about the incident.

The look of heartbreak, disappointment and shame on her face was more than I could bear at the time; although even after having witnessed how much my actions had hurt my Mother it didn't slow me down when the next chance came to me to commit an illegal activity. Can there be any more clear indications of an addict than this type of thought process?

What astounds me, even today, is how light the punishment through the courts was. I often wonder if I had received proper retribution would that not have aided me in going straight. Instead of proper disciplinary action I was placed on six months' probation and given the choice of either drawing a poster that would warn other kids about such actions or eight hours of community service.

My Mother, who accompanied me to the Parole officer, demanded that whatever the sternest reparation was available is what I deserved. At least she displayed some common sense which is more than I can say for the juvenile court system of the time.

I had such great success in finding that fix through car hopping that it wasn't long before my friend and I were back at it. Only this next time we didn't find keys. We came across a van in an alley close to another friends' house where we found a flat of beer.

What better way we thought to prove our manhood than to continue breaking into vehicles while intoxicated. Between the two of us we finished off the twenty-four cans of beer in short order. Neither one of us was especially fond of the taste but that was certainly not something we would share with the other.

Thus I found the ultimate rush, adrenalin mixed with a mind-altering substance. I cannot relay the remainder of that evening as I was far to inebriated to remember. All I can recall is an evening of drunkenness, fighting and looking in cars.

It was as if that evening was a new birth. I had found that for which I was searching. Being part of a group that committed these illegal activities made me feel a sense of belonging. Not backing down in the face of danger gave me a sense of worth and pride. The adrenalin was a drug unto itself and when it was mixed with alcohol, and later as I learned drugs, I had apparently found the perfect combination.

With drugs, an addict needs to continue searching for a better high, or at least a way to duplicate the euphoria you experience when you first try a drug. Heroin users call it "Chasing the Dragon" always in search of the original buzz.

Whether it is a stronger drug or simply taking more of your drug of choice the search doesn't end until you overdose, or quit. This was the case for me with both the drugs and my illegal activity. As I will relay to you later on, my forays into the criminal world became far more aggressive and far more dangerous. Now that I am clean from drugs, I can look back on those days with gratitude in my heart that I am here to write this.

Chapter 4

"A Wake Up Call"

Certain names have been changed to protect both the innocent and the guilty but more importantly to protect me from both.

I firmly believe that when we embark upon a destructive path God will often send us hints that we should rethink our actions. In my experience these suggestions range from gentle nudges to firm smacks in the head.

What follows is an example of the latter, unfortunately I wasn't listening at the time and in fact it took many, many more such hints to wake me up.

Sam's brother Derrick was several years older than Sam. He was generally mean, unsavory and therefore epitomized the type of person, for some delusional reason, I wanted to emulate.

Derrick's legendary status among our group was sealed the day when another friend of ours displayed his talent for running his mouth until Derrick smacked the smile off his face; although I now abhor such displays of violence, based upon ignorance at the time, I thought this friend of ours got what he deserved, but what really sealed Derrick's reputation was what followed.

Our now less mouthy friend ran from the house we were in screaming that "His Dad was a f'ing meatpacker and he was going to send him back to kick Derrick's ass". At the time none of us thought it was more than one person trying to reduce their embarrassment. That was until shortly after his father did arrive, threatening all of us but especially Derrick. He stormed into the house and at once all of us knew we were going to witness some real violence.

However none of us foresaw what was about to happen. Without hesitation Derrick proceeded to trounce our friend's father, slapping him around without any real difficulty. After a short beating our friend's father made a hasty retreat.

Regardless of the fact that many of us had been in violent situations before this event shattered our still childlike ideal that fathers were somehow superhuman. Here was someone whom we associated with that seemed too had somehow risen above the confines of normality and had challenged the traditional beliefs.

Given my apparent low morality I saw this as cool beyond belief. I found myself craving the same ability to put fear into people. I know now that I was starting to mistake fear for respect.

After this incident many of us wouldn't hesitate to hang around with Derrick so it was without a second thought that following summer Sam and I drove in my car with Derrick to a smaller City north of where we lived. Derrick had taken up residence in this city and through his contacts with a certain group of gentleman that shared a similar interest in motorcycle riding had quickly become one of the larger mushroom dealers.

Derrick's gimmick was melting large amounts of chocolate, mixing in the mushrooms and freezing the concoction in cookie cutters, then selling the cookies at bars. Sam and I spent several days following Derrick from bar to bar, regardless of the fact we were underage, since the bouncers received payoffs to look the other way when Derrick was doing business they didn't seem to care about the fact Sam and I were obviously not supposed to be in this type of establishment.

As such I got my first taste of drug dealing. The people I met through this seemed to me to have no cares. They would settle any disagreement quickly, usually with violence. Through Derrick I started to associate with the wrong kind of role models.

I saw the type of fear they commanded, how people would give them a wide berth and would bend over backwards not to disagree with them, especially to their face. I saw how the groups of these types of people always backed each other up, or at least so I thought. I saw the money and also mistakenly associated money with success and happiness.

After several days of hanging out in seedy bars and befriending all sorts of less than reputable people we celebrated our apparent success with a party. Never before had I been in the company of so many rough people, bikers, dealers and hangers-on circulated through the house and it seemed that each and every one of them accepted us as equals. Never were we disrespected even though we were wide eyed at the experience and obviously several years younger than everyone else.

While Sam and I were sitting on the stairs talking about what a great time this was Derrick approached us: "You guys did great work, here have this and have fun". Both of us looked upon the largest bag of mushrooms we had seen.

I remember there was no hesitation from either of us as we both grabbed for the bag and started choking down mushrooms as fast as we could. Magic Mushrooms are very awful tasting but the situation reminded me of the first time I was offered a sip of beer although I hated the taste I certainly tried not to show it for fear of ridicule., I wanted to appear cool and used to situations that presented me with copious amount of drugs and so I fought back the need to gag and vomit each time I swallowed more mushrooms.

Although to this day I don't know exactly how much each of us consumed I can say with great certainty it was far too much. After a short amount of time Derrick came back to us giggling with amazement at how much we had eaten.

I interpreted this as acceptance, somehow as a sign that I had the merit to associate with these people, at the time I didn't know the hell I was soon to enter.

When you are on mushrooms you have no sense of time, in addition to the hallucinations, the giggles and feeling that everything and everyone has taken on a certain surreal quality five minutes will seem like an eternity and feel like it has passed in the blink of an eye all at once.

Although I had experimented with both acid and mushrooms long before this party I had never taken so much. My first real indication that perhaps I had exceeded the quantity my body was able to handle came when sitting in a bean bag in the living room listening to music I started to feel as if my body were floating.

Soon I thought I was floating on the bars of music. In my state I was sure I was levitating across the living room supported by the now visible bars of music that accompanied my macabre dance.

All of my fellow party members seemed to disappear and soon it seemed like it was only me and the music in the room. After several minutes of this I did the worst thing you can do, I started to panic. Immediately I could feel my heart rate increase, I broke out into a sweat and then came the paranoia.

I was consumed with a sense that everyone in the house knew I was messed up. I was certain I could see them all staring at me, giggling behind their hands about this dumb kid. I was convinced that I could hear several of those in other rooms discussing my plight and asking Derrick why he had invited me there in the first place.

Gathering myself as best I could I ran to the bathroom and tried to lock myself in. I thought that somehow this smaller space would protect me from the evils of the drug, but I was totally incorrect. The bathroom became a prison, I vomited several times and continued to feel my heart rate increase, and soon I was convinced I was going to die.

In truth I do not know how long I stayed in the bathroom, I believe that several times people tried to enter the room only to find it locked. I wonder to this day if they even knew there was a very scarred kid on the other side of the door and that their knocks sounded like thunder. Regardless of how gently they tried the doorknob to me it sounded as if they were trying to break down the door and thereby only reinforcing my fears that Derrick was going to thrash me for ruining his party.

Perhaps even drag me out into the living room to parade me around those people I thought I had been accepted by to show this silly little boy off and all could get a good laugh.

Finally I screwed up enough nerve to leave the washroom and there at the top of the stairs I found Derrick. I tried to make normal conversation with him but his voice sounded as if someone had slowed down a record and therefore only served to freak me out more, what happened next sent me over the edge.

After talking to Derrick I went outside trying to convince myself I wasn't going to die and all I needed was the cool night air to help me. To my horror Derrick was there already. I asked him how he got outside so fast and he only gave me a weird look and asked sarcastically if "I thought the mushrooms had kicked in yet." I know now that I was hallucinating but at the time I couldn't make sense of how Derrick could be in two places at once.

To confirm this I immediately ran back into the house and up the stairs, knowing for certain Derrick hadn't followed. I freaked out when in my state I was sure I found him where I had left him at the top of the stairs.

At that point I knew I was in trouble. I went back outside convinced I had to get to a hospital and fast. Even in this state I was afraid of what anyone would say if they knew I was losing it and so I refused to ask anyone to drive me. Knowing what I do now about these types of people, myself included, I probably would have been better off trying to fly to the hospital than ask one of them to risk getting in trouble driving a minor to get medical attention.

Displaying the type of self-centered behavior that is typical with addicts I jumped into my car and headed out to the hospital, not even stopping to think about the potential of hurting or killing someone since I was in no shape to drive.

I turned on the radio hoping it would calm me but it had the opposite effect as the music sounded like chipmunks were singing. I immediately turned it off. Realizing for the first time it was raining

I turned on the wipers. Unfortunately one of the side effects of a hallucinogenic is what is referred to as "strobing". You can wave your hand in front of your face and it appears as if several hands follow it. Now imagine this effect when starring through a windshield with a large rubber stick traveling across your vision. Without hesitation I turned off the wipers deciding to just deal with the rain.

I do not remember the drive to the hospital and to this day thank God I didn't hurt anyone. Luckily for me the hospital was not crowded and I was seen right away, given how I must have looked, sweating, panicked and obviously under the influence of some drug I am certain I was truly seen as an emergency.

The Doctor questioned me for some time as to what I had taken but I feared reprisal from Derrick and so tried to concoct some story that I was at a bar, left my beer unattended than shortly after finishing it started to feel "funny". He knew I was lying but apparently decided not to push it. I am sure that by looking into my eyes he could tell it was mushrooms or acid, given the size of my pupils.

After hooking me to a heart monitor the Doctor admonished me for being high and pointed out that my heart was dangerously close to giving out. I remember him telling me that without medical attention I would have probably been dead by morning. He then gave me a pill, probably Ativan, and told me that should help bring me down. Eventually it took four of these pills to bring me to a point where I didn't think I was going to die.

While I was waiting for the medication to kick in I distinctly remember an orderly coming into the room and in a kindly voice saying "So took a little too much tonight did you?" He then proceeded to sit with me, even at times holding my hand reassuring me that I would be just fine and that he would stay with me until I felt better. For an immeasurable amount of time he did just that. He stayed with me and was instrumental in helping me relax and allow the medication to work.

Soon after he left the room the Doctor came back to check on me. So impressed by the care and attention I had received from the orderly, I commented to the Doctor how much this hospital employee had helped.

He looked at me for several moments and then finally said "There are no orderlies on staff tonight. The only ones that have seen you are me and the nurse". I was stunned but decided not press the issue further fearing they might commit me.

Although the presence of the orderly could be explained away by the fact I may have still been hallucinating, I prefer to believe that perhaps a guardian angel was sent to help me. Believing that gives me strength today knowing that if I was spared from such an end there must be bigger and better things planned for me in the future.

Unfortunately as you will read later it took several more brushes with death and despairing situations for me to "Hit Bottom".

It is my hope someone will read this and not see it as a glorification of the life or the effects of drugs but rather for the depiction of depravity and senselessness that it truly represents.

Chapter 5

"Fatal Coolness"

In retrospect there is absolutely no doubt in my mind that I was just as addicted to the lifestyle as I was to the drugs. The constant adrenalin rush mixed with fear gave me a rush that was only ever superseded by narcotics.

As such, associating with people who were infamous in this world allowed me to not only gain notoriety but also get even that much closer to the lifestyle itself.

The first person of such character I started hanging out with was a drug dealer named Dragon. Dragon was the main supplier of cocaine in our city and therefore he was well known and feared.

I first met Dragon in a bar, a bar that seemed not to notice I was several years under age; either that or they simply didn't care. Soon I found myself playing a game of pool against one of the scariest individuals I had ever laid eyes on.

Dragon stood easily six foot five and looked as if he was a professional wrestler; his demeanor was that of a person you simply would not mess with. His attitude towards those that clung to him was of open disdain; yet I noticed that no matter how poorly he treated them they continued to do his bidding.

After a few games I was invited back to his table where I met his two main bill collectors. Lucky and Smitty both seemed as ominous as Dragon and spoke very little. In fact Lucky came across as more of a lapdog for Dragon; eagerly awaiting his master's approval.

Smitty was just the opposite; instantaneously I knew he was the type of person that would rather put a bullet in your head than have to argue with you.

I never knew why Dragon took such an interest in me. As I said it certainly wasn't that he didn't have enough hangers-on. Over the next several months I would often receive lessons directly from Dragon on how to profit on the street, how to enforce your reputation and most importantly how to ensure you were able to maintain your territory. A lesson to which, unfortunately for Dragon, he should have paid more attention.

Approximately six months after meeting Dragon and living the high life I was being seen all over town with him and his henchmen. It finally got to the point where I was being recognized by the police even when alone. At the time I couldn't believe the rush I would get from this association. Here I was a kid for all intense and purposes and yet because of who I was hanging around with, I considered myself untouchable.

However it wasn't long until the life caught up to Dragon as it always does. If I have learned one thing through my experiences, it is that the bill always comes due. You can try and run or hide from it but without fail someday you will have to pay. Too often the payment required is death.

The city police had enough of Dragon's notoriety and finally decided to bring him down. As with most people caught up in this life, the easiest way is to find someone to rat them out. Someone more interested in saving their own skin or reducing their sentence on whatever charges they are facing than keeping their mouths shut.

Although I am proud to say I am out of this type of life, the rat still bothers me.

Unfortunately for Dragon the rat the police were able to coerce into flipping was Lucky, Dragon's right hand man. Soon Dragon was arrested and behind bars. Although Lucky had also been arrested he was already back out on the street.

It didn't take long for people to realize just exactly what had happened and everyone was amazed that Lucky remained in town. Perhaps he thought that with Dragon in jail he had nothing to fear. He was wrong, dead wrong!

Dragon had all the resources that came with being a fairly high level drug dealer. One of these resources was money, lots of it and with that money he was able to get out on bail, unbeknownst to Lucky.

The final few scenes of Lucky's life weren't as dramatic as you may expect. When Dragon and Smitty entered the bar that Lucky was in, a look of resignation passed over his face. Without saying a word he got up and left the bar with his two previous cohorts.

Several days later it was reported in the local newspaper that a known drug dealer who went by the name Lucky was found on a beach in a neighboring province with several bullet holes in him.

Lucky's bill had come due.

It wasn't long after that that things started to unravel, as they always do, for Dragon and Smitty. An Asian gang set their eyes on Dragon's territory and soon he and Smitty disappeared. Some say they fled the country ahead of prosecution but most believe if you really want to find them you better bring a shovel.

With Dragon gone I was without a role model, and yes I use the term role model with great sarcasm. Yet with my ability to fit into any crowd in almost any situation, it wasn't long before I found a new person to teach me the ins and outs of the street life. In the grand scheme of things it was apparent I was moving up the ladder as my newfound leader was a highly decorated and high ranking member of a local motor bike gang. At the time I was working for a home location service when Brent came in. Immediately I knew that he was the type of person I related to or at least thought I did. His mannerisms, his speech all spoke of unquestioned authority and his stature said he could back up his directions. After going out of my way to find him a place to live I was soon invited to his house where he supplied marijuana, booze, hash, pretty much anything I wanted free of charge. Soon I became a regular at the club house, hanging around the type of people that most would cross the street to avoid and yet I felt at home, accepted, a part of something bigger than myself.

Through this entire relationship I was never asked to do anything illegal. It was never a condition of my presence to get involved in any activity for which I didn't volunteer.

Day by day, much like with Dragon, I learned how to carry myself in certain situations. I saw what happened to people who crossed Brent and how devastating he was in dishing out his punishment.

Brent was feared and I wanted to be feared as well.

With most organizations like this, their main supply of income is drug dealing; so once again I had found a group of people to hang around with that not only showed me the way of the street, took care of me but also supplied my addiction. I guess you could say they were looking after all of my addictions.

As with most addicts I was leading a double life. I was not aware of how deep of a hole I was digging for myself. During the day I was working nine to five at a respectable job that had great potential for advancement. By night I was seeking out and hanging out in the most infamous locations I could with the most notorious people

It wasn't until later associations that I learned that way too often the people I was hanging out with would eventually expect me to earn my keep. It still amazes me to this day how street wise I was becoming and yet so naïve to the true motives of some of the individuals I met along my travels.

Not long after meeting Brent I was transferred to California through my work. Although there are other incidents that happened before my move and certainly a lot that happened in California we will discuss those later.

After being away for quite a while I came back to my hometown only to turn on the news and see Brent. The news was reporting that he had just been identified as the provincial leader of a far more infamous and dangerous motorcycle gang. Did I feel guilt for my association with this criminal? Did it occur to me that through my dealings with this group of individuals I had to take a certain responsibility for their actions? Even if my only involvement in the actual activities was that of complicity, No! No! The only thing I felt at the time was pride. Pride that I knew this person and could call on him anytime I wanted.

As with Dragon, Brent's bill came due. He is now serving ten to fifteen years in a maximum security prison for murder. Once again you would think that perhaps this would dissuade me from seeking out such relationships; but the opposite was true. I knew someone who had murdered someone else and even more importantly, people knew that I knew him.

With all that I had learned from these people and many more that I haven't written about it wasn't long until I was putting the lessons I had learned into practice. Person by person I soon gathered a group of likeminded people around me that were interested in the same things - Money, fear and drugs.

Before too long we were becoming well known, almost too well known. We were often stopped at random by the police to search us or to see if the particular car we were driving was stolen. We sold drugs as often as possible and although we certainly didn't ever get to the level of sales of the people I have mentioned, we thought we were successful. Most dangerously we thought we were hard. Since those days I have dealt with real gang members. People who would shoot you for wearing the wrong colored shirt or bandana or simply for being in the wrong neighborhood.

The real gang members I later met cared nothing for life and never showed any remorse in taking it.

However as I said, at the time we thought we were tough, and in many situations those who dealt with us thought the same. A local night club became our main hang out and after a while not even the bouncers or the owners dared to question anything we wanted to do in the bar.

One particular night people that were not in our regular circle came into the bar and started causing a disturbance. The bouncers actually asked us to do something about it. So after a few minutes of verbal jousting all of us, approximately twenty people, took the problem outside.

At that time it was rumored that I in particular carried a gun. Although I didn't, I certainly did nothing to dissuade people from this belief. So as the fracas broke out and all mayhem ensued, a few of the combatants recognized me and started to retreat thinking they may get shot. What a perverted sense of strength this gave me.

We chased them across the parking lot laying a beating on anyone that wasn't fast enough to get away. That night I saw the inexplicable ugliness of violence and for some demented reason at the time I enjoyed it.

After that our reputation grew by leaps and bounds, which isn't always a good thing. Usually neighboring gangs will hear of your activities and if you're making money decide to take over. However we were lucky. We were allowed to carry out our day to day business of intimidating people, selling whatever drugs we didn't use ourselves and flaunting the law.

Near the end we became so brazen that when one night we were offered cash for new tires if we could somehow procure them we simply walked a couple of blocks away from the bar hoisted a car up on blocks and simply stole all four tires. Once again proving that the majority of us had lost touch with any sense of morality.

It is my true desire that someone reading this will not see it as glamorization. They will see through the supposed coolness of it and see it for what it is a one-way road that leads to either death or jail.

Perhaps as you read this you can associate with it and see for yourself the hole you are digging. Maybe this will give you enough warning to get out of that hole before someone starts throwing dirt on you.

Chapter 6

"Behind Bars"

Hindsight being twenty-twenty, I should have easily seen the natural progression of my activities leading me to jail, as they did.

As with most addictions one must forever increase the amount that it takes to provide the desired effect. It is the same with adrenalin, no longer was I reacting the same way from minor drug deals and stealing cars.

Being considered part of the group you didn't want to mess with at a local night club and even earning such a reputation as I did with both the police and those on the street no longer seemed to provide the same escape it once had.

I must admit that while going through all of these activities the fear of getting caught or the possible negative consequences never occurred to me. In fact the closer I came to getting caught the more I enjoyed the activity.

Therefore when I wound up being arrested and having to be booked into a jail for the first time it was an eye opening experience, at least at first.

That night started like most, several of us gathered at a friend's house. We were smoking pot, some drinking, when suddenly one of the members of our group mentioned a local gas station that was closed and how he was sure we could quickly gain access and remove a large amount of cigarettes.

As it is now cigarettes can earn you a fair asking price on the street. Suddenly it felt like I was awake again. Here was an opportunity to not only take part in something I had never done before but it also upped the ante, I knew I was moving into a whole new realm of illegal activity and therefore a whole new level of adrenalin.

It didn't take long for us to formulate a plan; of course at the time we considered ourselves high level criminals and therefore who needed to plan? We were all sure we could easily get into the gas station, remove what we wanted and slip into the night.

I can barely type that paragraph without seeing how incredibly dumb the thought process at the time was.

We decided that "Penguin", a rather chubby member of our group and I would get into the store while several others would wait close by in a car for a quick escape.

As we approached the gas station I thought I was on cloud nine, the adrenalin pumping through my body was incredible. It seemed that every sensation in my body was heightened to a level I had never felt before. There were no thoughts of how stupid this was or what would happen if I got caught.

Our first point of attempted entry was the back door. Both of us knew that the store would be alarmed and quickly decided that Penguin would open the door and enter the gas station while I stayed at the door retrieving the bags of cigarettes and watching outside for anyone coming.

I can still clearly remember how everything seemed so quiet that night. The air had a specific smell that is hard to describe but to this day I identify that smell with trouble.

At the time everything seemed perfect, crisp, and clear almost as if the world was in such awe of my activities it had stopped to watch.

We tried for several minutes at the back door and apart from causing significant damage we accomplished nothing. We certainly were a long way from the slick progression through our plan that we had foreseen.

Finally both of us got frustrated and that is when Penguin simply went to the side of the building and using the crowbar we had brought, smashed in the window. I was in shock! This didn't seem secretive or quiet. This was brash and apparently ill-fated.

Penguin entered the store and immediately started to fill up the garbage bags we had with us passing them through the window to me. During this operation I cut my arm on a piece of glass. Cutting my arm was an occurrence that I would later come to deeply regret.

After retrieving several bags we ran into the night, sprinting into the designated alley we found the others waiting, everyone seemed pumped up on the adrenalin that I alone thought I was feeling. We tore into the night making jokes about each other's actions everyone rapt with attention as Penguin and I described in great and probably exaggerated detail our exploits.

For that moment we were heroes and even now I must shake my head at the misguided sense of priorities that allowed anyone to see someone who had just committed a crime as a hero or who could possibly accept such accolade as deserving.

The idea was to return to our friend's house and count the loot as it were. It didn't take long for the police to react. On the way back we saw several police cruisers circulating through the area obviously believing that those responsible were on foot.

The worst moment came when we were stopped at a red light and a police van pulled up beside us. Instantly all conversation in the car died as each of in turn came to the sudden realization this may not go as well as we had hoped.

The van was larger than our car so although I kept sneaking looks at the police I couldn't see in their windows. This fact is probably what saved us from getting arrested right there and then. Since we couldn't see in their windows they couldn't see in ours and therefore didn't see the bags of cigarettes we were trying to hide.

After what seemed like an eternity the light turned green, the police van turned down a side street and there was a collective sigh from all of us in the car. Eventually we made it back to the house and once again our spirits were high as we entered.

That's when we found out that Sam had shot himself with a pellet gun while we were gone. Usually this would have been the source of great amusement. That Sam having been intensely intoxicated had wondered what it would feel like to put the gun to his hand and fire.

Given Sam's ramblings when we entered, apparently it didn't feel all that good. Upon closer examination we could see the pellet pushing up on the skin on the other side of his hand. The pellet had almost gone entirely through his hand.

Most of us wouldn't have given this a second thought. We probably would have told anyone else that they were retarded, deserved this and should find their own way to get medical attention. However this was Sam and he had been with the group almost since its inception.

As such we decided someone had to drive Sam to the hospital.

Rather than choosing someone to take him we all jumped into the car and headed to the hospital. The wait was unusually short and soon our friend was being seen by a doctor

That was the point when things really started to fall apart. Apparently someone sitting close to us overheard two things, gas station robbery and gunshot wound. They took it upon themselves to call the police.

Before the police arrived I had decided to give one of my friends a ride home. We had transferred the cigarettes into my car and I left with him. After dropping him off the thought did cross my mind that perhaps I should hide the goods somewhere. However I didn't pay heed to this logical thought and carried on to the hospital. As soon as I walked into the main entrance I knew something was wrong, I was halfway down the hall when I glanced over my shoulder and noticed two city policeman quietly following me. Instantly I knew I was busted.

Calmly I found the rest of my crew and sat down with them. One of the officers approached me and said "You must be Mr _ _ _ _" to which I responded "Yes". My heart had already sunk into my stomach, which was doing flips at the time. The craziest thing was that even in this intense moment of not knowing what was about to happen or how much trouble I was in; I was simply enjoying the rush.

He asked me if I knew anything about a gas station that been robbed earlier that night. Of course I answered "No" and put on my best "I'm innocent" face, he replied "Well the odd thing is it seems you have a nasty cut on your arm and there was blood left on the window of the store"

Figuring out pretty quickly I was caught I said "I might know something about that".

"I'm glad to hear you say that, since we already have all the details of the crime, your name and address and what part you played. This was supplied to us by your friend, uhm the one you call Penguin".

I was in shock! I couldn't believe how quickly this supposed streetwise person had given me up; I turned to Sam with an inquisitive look on my face as if to ask "Is this true". He just looked me deep in the eye and nodded once.

I was incensed! How could someone who had assisted in the act and in fact had come up with the idea be so quick to throw in the towel on those around him?

I have always figured that when you're busted, you're busted. I have seen way too many people make similar situations worse by continuing to lie, or even worse yet resisting arrest. At this point I knew the game was over.

Soon I was taken into a room to be seen by a doctor to have my arm sewn up. The whole time the officer persisted in his questioning asking; "Who else's idea was it" and "How did you get away from the scene so quickly?" "Were you driving and if so who else was involved"

He went on to ask about the involvement of Sam and I told him the truth that Sam had stayed behind and too no part in the illegal activity.

As I said, although I was less than cooperative, not wanting to hang myself further I wasn't disrespectful to the officer knowing he was simply doing his job. I have also learned that if you treat the police with respect you often get that respect returned regardless of the circumstances.

Soon it was time to be taken in for booking. I must have developed a rapport with the arresting officers because I was led out of the hospital without handcuffs; whereas Penguin was fully cuffed. I even went so far at one point as we approached the police car to ask "Can I drive?" the officer laughed and said "Not this time."

We were both taken downtown. I spent my time glaring daggers at Penguin and trying to communicate that the first chance I got to get even I was going to take full advantage of it. After processing, the removal of our eyewear, shoelaces and belts we were placed in separate holding tanks.

At the time that was one of the longest nights of my life. There were several others in the holding cell, most of whom looked ready to fight at a moment's notice. I had never been in this situation before but knew enough to immediately strike up a friendly conversation with the largest guy in the cell.

Obviously I had no intention of becoming his bitch but I figured if the crap hit the fan that night I was staying close to this guy. Luckily for me I was able to adapt to the circumstances and relate at least on some level with most of the people in the cell, as such I had no problems that evening.

The following morning I was given a public defender that was able to get me released on my own recognizance (ROR). I immediately went home. Obviously my family knew I was gone the entire night and although they were used to me being out very late, staying out all night was something new.

I told them I had gotten into a fight at a bar because someone was harassing my girlfriend and so I had to defend her. For the time being the lie worked. They certainly didn't approve of violence but as my Dad said "How much can you take, if someone is harassing your girlfriend, before you do something?"

It wasn't long before I was scouring the streets looking for Penguin and looking for retribution. Sadly enough at the time, there was only one way I knew how to handle his betrayal and that way would probably get me in a lot more trouble. I made several calls explaining to those I knew what he had done and to keep an eye out for him. It wasn't until after several days of intensive searching that I learned he had not been released as I had because he had several warrants out for his arrest and therefore would be held until the trial date.

Months went by and I stuck to my lie about how I was in trouble due to a fight and never mentioned the gas station. My parents are not dumb people and soon realized there was something wrong with my story.

When the trial finally arrived, without me knowing it, they sent my eldest brother to the court that morning to read the court docket and find out exactly what I was in trouble for.

I had arrived a few hours before my scheduled hearing and that is when I finally saw Penguin. He didn't see me as he entered the bathroom in the concourse of the courthouse. I was almost giddy and also wired from the expected adrenalin. This was my chance as I saw it, to put things straight. I would follow him into the bathroom and if he was alone, I was going to clearly demonstrate my dislike of rats.

As I entered the bathroom I noticed Penguin washing his hands, and to my surprise he was in fact the only other person there. Immediately a vision of me smashing his head through the mirror came to mind and I stepped forward to put that plan into action. As I approached him I asked "So how does it feel to be a rat, bitch?

I got ready to leap at him when all of a sudden an extremely calm voice behind me said "You don't really want to do that Mr _ _ _ _ _." "It will only end you up in a lot more trouble."

Whirling around I saw the officer who had originally arrested me. Apparently he had seen me follow Penguin into the bathroom and knew exactly what I was going to do.

He escorted me from the bathroom, took me into court and sat there with me until my case was called. From that point on he never said a word to me.

The evidence was given. I pleaded no contest and was given probation, since it was my first crime as an adult, and ordered to pay restitution.

I would be remiss in not divulging another secret I have held. Soon after the trial I found out that Penguin was being sent to a minimum security prison and I just happened to know someone who was going there as well. I made certain that this other friend of mine made it a priority to spread the word that Penguin was a rat. From what I understood Penguin's time was not easy time.

I never did see Penguin after that and in fact most of the group's members slipped off to do their own thing shortly after, unfortunately most of those things included jail time and for some real unfortunates death.

Looking back on the incident I am amazed at how quickly one can slide into this type of activity. Whether it is due to drug addiction, adrenalin addiction or simply following the crowd, it seems so easy for people to take the wrong path.

Often when we start on the wrong path it seems so difficult to get off of it even when that is what we want to do. Another thing is that I have been blessed by people, sometimes strangers that help me. Examine the officer, because I treated him with respect I was not embarrassed by being led out of the hospital in handcuffs. Even more significantly, he was there when my actions could have landed me in jail for three to five years and had the presence of mind to stop me.

I believe that these types of people are placed in our lives to give us a helping hand when we need it. I pray that I will always keep my eyes open for them and that if they arrive to help me that I will be accepting.

Chapter 7

"California Dreaming"

California, the place where dreams come true. The land of potential; or so I thought. Shortly after completing my probation time for the break and enter I found a respectable job working in home location and property management.

Although they treated us new recruits as slaves it finally gave me a sense of direction and I excelled at the position. A lot of my extracurricular activities remained but as I progressed through the company I found I became less and less interested in testing the boundaries.

After a while I was approached by management and asked if I wanted to go to California to head up the opening of two new offices - one in Oakland and one in Concord.

I was still a young kid, so this type of opportunity seemed like one I simply couldn't pass up. Without much hesitation I agreed. In an amazingly short amount of time I was packed and sent to California.

Talk about culture shock! No amount of time on the street or hanging out with those I did while at home, could have prepared me for the experiences I was about to go through. It is fortunate to some extent that I at least had some street sense at this point; as soon that hard learned knowledge would be put to the test.

I distinctly remember walking out of the airport and immediately smelling the same pungent odor I had that night we broke into the gas station. It smelled like trouble, I was filled with a sense of incredible adventure.

The regional manager of the company met me at the airport, introduced himself as Alex, and told me that I would be in charge of both of the new offices, reporting only to him.

All other employees, those already working for the company and those yet to be hired, would be reporting directly to me. Talk about an ego boost. A 19 year old being told he was second in charge for the two offices in California and that, even though half the employees were at least twice his age, they would all be under his guidance.

I couldn't wait to start. This was a new beginning. A chance to leave behind all the trouble I had made back home; although at the time I felt as if it was trouble others were making for me. At that point I wasn't up on the concept of taking responsibility for my own actions.

Due to the criminal record, I had to sneak into the country and was told I would be paid under the table. As far as any official was concerned or informed, I was simply there for a friend's wedding.

Although this dubious start did in fact take some of the polish off my sense of rebirth; I stuffed the unease and moved forward, concentrating on only the positive.

Alex and I toured through Oakland for several hours. He educated me on the neighborhoods that I should avoid at all costs; which ones were safe, at least during the day and of course those that I could feel secure being in.

It was right out of a movie and I felt like the main actor. It was almost as if I had moved from a hick town to the big city. Like on television I saw open drug deals, fights, prostitutes, boarded up buildings, entire walls covered in gang insignia.

It wasn't as if most of these things were new to me; but the concentration of the sightings and the general aura produced an almost intoxicating effect. One must remember I had always been drawn to areas and people who were dangerous and here seemed to be the Mecca of such a place. To some degree it seemed as if I had come home and I couldn't wait to get my feet wet.

Eventually our tour wound down and we headed back to the hotel where we would be living until we found an apartment for which the company would pay. Alex and I, being upper management, were afforded a respectable allowance to procure somewhere to live.

As we walked up the stairs to the hotel Alex stopped me and asked "Do you smoke?" Having smoked cigarettes for years and completely missing what he was driving at, I said "Yes."

"No" He said "Do you **smoke**?" Understanding dawned on me that he was referring to marijuana. To this day it amazes me that even though an hour ago I was fixated on this fresh chance, I didn't hesitate to admit that I enjoyed marijuana, knowing full well what it would lead to, elimination of the new beginning.

After I had answered his question in the positive, Alex with a straight face said "Well we don't abide that, you're fired! Find your own way home." I was stunned! How the hell was I suddenly going to find cash to make it all the way back to Canada?

That's when I noticed Alex was smiling. Apparently it was funny to him to scare the crap out of me. I forced a laugh and we proceeded upstairs.

That is when things got weird.

As I got settled in Alex started to roll a joint. Calmly he turned to me and asked "Have you ever tried a cocoa puff" I had no clue what this was and told him so. "Well you mix a line of cocaine in the marijuana and smoke it that way." "It's far more intense than just the pot."

Holy crap what had I stumbled into? Even after all the drugs I had tried, most to excess, I have never tried cocaine. In my younger years hanging around Dragon I saw the effects it could have on those that used it. People selling everything they had just so they could get that next line. All in search of that next high.

So of course knowing this I immediately turned down the cocaine and told him how offended I was at the suggestion, right? No, of course not. I wanted to fit in and I found myself not wanting to admit my naivety even to this stranger. I just couldn't shake the thought process that I had to appear tough and dangerous even in front of someone I didn't even know.

I accepted the cocoa puff and smoked my share. For quite a while I was surprised that there didn't seem to be any different affect from the addition of cocaine to the marijuana and that is when it hit me. A sensation of total release, it was as if I had never had any problems in my life. Any misgivings I had about the move were gone. Everything in the room took on a brand new significance.

In that moment the best way I can describe the sensation was that I had just met God. Of course at that point I had no idea of the unavoidable pitfalls that awaited me, if I continued. At that moment there was no future, no plans. There was only the moment at hand and my newly damaged brain thought that moment was the epitome of perfection.

I was enveloped in a sensation of comforting warmth. The confidence I felt was such that I had never experienced before. Every doubt I had about moving to a new country and taking on a job, which I wasn't sure I was qualified to take; all the homesickness I felt, all the self-doubts about my own abilities, were gone.

The rest of the night slipped by in a haze. Although I was offered more I didn't take any. So perfect did the buzz seem at the time that I didn't want to wreck it.

However the next day there was a brand new sensation as I awoke; a need for the same feeling I'd had last night. At that point it was easily justifiable. I had closed my mind to the negatives and had easily convinced myself that this new wonder drug could answer all of life's problems.

After the first try at cocaine I was already demonstrating serious addictive behaviors.

For the next few weeks we progressed as normal. I negotiated a fairly good compensation package that included my accommodation. It was especially beneficial given the fact that I was being paid under the table and therefore didn't have to pay tax.

Periodically we would use cocaine and each time we did I found it more difficult to quit for the night also I was usually first to start using the next time we partook. With cocaine the need to increase the amount you are taking quickly increases. Soon each session not only becomes longer, happens at different times of day but each time the amount consumed increases.

Being in the state I was when using, I either didn't notice or didn't care.

As in most situations like this, I started to meet the people from whom we were buying. As had happened before, I was drawn to these people; actually preferring to spend my time with them than those with whom I worked.

That was unless, of course, those I worked with had free drugs for me. I was quickly learning the manipulative way of the addict. It amazes me how quickly I gravitated to the most dangerous people I could find.

One specific dealer had major gang connections and would actually receive shipment of kilos of cocaine on his boat at the docks or out in the Bay. It didn't take long before I was accompanying him to some of these buys. Although I knew that some of the stories of drug deals gone bad and people getting killed were real and often expected; how could I pass up the adrenalin rush that awaited such a trip?

We met with black and Asian gang members, even spending time with some of them as we partied or celebrated our deal. You have to know that although for a lot of the time I was scared beyond reason as these transactions took place; I could never overcome the sensation and enjoyment that I was part of this major deal.

The main dealer was a guy called "Frog." Frog got his name early in life while trying to set up his own territory of drug dealing. He had been confronted by a rival dealer and a fight ensued. During the altercation Frog was hit in the throat with a led pipe crushing his voice box.

The scary thing? Frog went on to not only win that fight but to also beat the rival to death. From that point on Frog's reputation was sealed. His voice sounded exactly like a frog. Over the next few years several people made the very real mistake of razzing him about his odd voice. After dealing with a few of these people, no one every teased him about it again.

The other two main dealers I was hanging around with were a husband and wife team, Two of the sleaziest people I had ever dealt with; but it is hard to be rational when they have what you need. It was these two that I eventually approached about a business opportunity; offering to help them increase the amount of stock and customers and thus increase the profits.

Only by the grace of God did everything fall apart before we could put this deal in place. Had I taken this step I honestly do not believe I would be here today to relay this story to you.

So here I was in another country. My days filled with creating the illusion of someone who was a hard worker. I was respected by most that worked for me. We quickly got the two offices up and running and profitable. My nights were filled with associating with the most hardened people and doing cocaine.

Soon most of those that worked with us were using cocaine as well. Sick people seem to gravitate towards sick people. Before long our group started to grow. As we all had money, there was always an ample supply of cocaine around. Although others drank or smoked marijuana in addition to the coke, I was fine with just the powder. Why would I want to depress this sense of ecstasy it was providing?

It wasn't long before the length of our parties started to affect our daily activities. I don't know how many times I went to work after an hour or two of sleep; or sometimes none at all. This formed a pattern that would continue to worsen.

It got to the point where I was doing cocaine at work. If I was ever caught by Alex the regional manager, all I had to do was offer him some. Usually it was him coming into the office and offering me some.

I was unaware how far Alex had already slipped by this point. I was oblivious to anything outside of the cocaine and he was never around. I noticed that my usage was actually changing my personality. I was quickly turning into a moody person, easy to offend. My employees quickly found I was turning from a person you could work for and respect into an asshole, for lack of a better term.

By this point I had only been in California for a few months and already I was getting to the point where my whole life centered around drugs and those that sold them. I was turning into someone to whom I would never have talked. I was avoiding contact with my family back home and I was losing sight of the opportunity that had first awaited me when I came to California.

Everyone involved was changing around me as well. Verbal fights became more and more frequent. The level of drama each new situation brought with it became almost unbearable. I corrected these situations with more cocaine.

I was learning that, rather than having to feel, I preferred to be in a drug induced haze.

Even the places we would hang out at night drastically changed. We started out frequenting reputable bars and night clubs. Within a couple of months however we were regulars at a seedy bar. The bar was situated on the wharf and was usually not a place the police frequented. That was unless they were there to investigate another stabbing or fight.

Each night offered something new at the bar. One night was reserved for the bikers, while the next might be for the local street gang. The druggies took Wednesday and so on and on it went. With some of these groups you really took your life in your hands stepping into the bar. However, being the good addict I was, I could manipulate most situations and most people to my favour. Soon I and those with me were welcomed, or at least tolerated by all the diverse groups that would go to the bar.

Perhaps the most important element was the fact we had money and they had what we wanted, drugs.

We continued going to this bar until one night we made the very real mistake of taking the president of the company there on one of his visits to Oakland.

It took about fifteen minutes before someone accused him of being a NARC and the fight was on. They were dragging him out of the bar and had we not jumped into action I am unsure in what shape he would have been found.

Luckily that was the night that the bikers were there; and already having got to know several we were able to dissuade those who were removing their next victim from the bar. I know it was not my amazing negotiating power that accomplished this; especially given the condition I was in, but rather the fact that a couple of those that I had enlisted were well known bikers. In addition to their reputation it was also well known they carried guns at all times.

I suppose at that point those that had decided the president of our company was actually a NARC took a second to realize that maybe he wasn't after all; and that messing with those standing before them wouldn't be advantageous to their health.

Man what a rush! To be able to enlist the help of people so feared that by them simply walking over to the situation and explaining this guy was with them it ended the crisis. To see the reaction, the immediate recognition of what waited for those that crossed the bikers was incredible and I wanted more.

Once again I had found a way to mix drug usage and associating with those people that would put me into situations for the greatest release of adrenalin. I thought I was all of that.

Even though I am clean today and thank God each day I am, there are times when I find myself almost missing situations like that. I seem to sometimes obsess about not only the drugs but also the life.

There is no doubt in my mind I have been given a chance to do something far more beneficial with my life. I have been spared the fate that happens to most in this type of life and I was allowed to live.

I know for a fact that there is a reason for the additional chances I received. I know also the blessing and the enormous gift involved in the second chances; yet there are times when like a ghost from the past a voice whispers in my ear "Remember how great it was!"

It is getting to the point now where I can say "No, it wasn't great. Having a clear head and a chance at a real life, that is great."

Most of all I am learning to take responsibility for my actions. No longer do I find it acceptable to blame others for the temptation they provided or the situations for which I felt they were to blame.

I alone am responsible for my actions and I am finding that only through this acceptance can I start to grow.

Chapter 8

"California Nightmare"

How quickly a new beginning can turn into a dead end; a dream into a nightmare. My time in California was relatively short and yet it only took me this limited time to accomplish my apparently subconscious goal of sabotaging most good things in my life.

This is not a statement of self-pity but rather a statement of the obvious pattern I have followed.

The cocaine use had quickly become all important. My friends, my career, even my family back at home took a back seat to my newfound obsession.

One incident that demonstrated this perfectly was when I forgot my older brother's birthday. I called him while high and asked him if he had received the shirt I had sent. Obviously this was a lie and no shirt was ever mailed.

It is funny how you remember these types of things when the regrets of the past visit you in your dreams.

It didn't take long before the usage of the cocaine and the costs associated, quickly exceeded my income. I had always heard horror stories of how people had snorted away large amounts of money, businesses and property but of course this would never apply to me.

The last year spent in California is even to this day hard to remember. So many of my memories of that time seem to be cast in a haze where details are blurred; yet there are events I do not think I will ever forget, no matter how hard I try.

Towards the end the group of us had become so deeply imbedded in a routine of drug use that when the end came none of us saw it approaching. One must keep in mind the effect cocaine has on someone. Everything else in your life is secondary, **everything**!

Todd, one of my employees, and I had become involved with local gang members who had originally used our property management service. We were supposed to be employed to protect the owners of the properties from certain clientele and wound up renting to the type of people they didn't want.

There was never any question as to the ultimate goal of the gang members and drug dealers. They had every intention of setting up these houses as gang hideouts or crack houses and we knew it.

One evening one of the gang members dropped by the office with payment for our services. The obvious payment we wanted was drugs. At the time we thought we were so clever. Regardless of any of our past experiences with people like this, we had actually convinced ourselves that we were the ones in control. It never occurred to us that we were being used and that the drugs provided only fueled our dependence on those we thought we were besting.

At any rate the gang member dropped off a sizeable baggie of white powder. I remember my disappointment when I learned that it wasn't cocaine but was in fact crank, more commonly referred to as speed.

Being the good, reliable and trustworthy addicts that we were both Todd and I quickly delved into the proceeds of the groups illegal activities and immediately tried what had been provided.

I must admit that when lost in my addiction there were very few drugs that at the time I didn't <u>think</u> I enjoyed, however this was one of them. The effect of the speed was like getting hit by a train, it seemed far faster acting and controlling.

As the rush hit me I could feel self-control and reason slipping away. Regardless of the fact that I knew I had just climbed on a virtually uncontrolled train to hell, I didn't care and so when it was again my turn I didn't hesitate.

Eventually Todd and I caught up to the group. Our condition at the time was obvious. Speed makes you sweat, makes you nervous and spotting someone under the influence of this drug is easy, especially to a fellow addict.

An argument broke out as to where we had obtained the drugs. Everyone knew it was supposed to be shared amongst the group, as it was allocated as proceeds from our combined efforts.

With a room full of addicts the quickest way to resolve confrontation is to offer drugs; so Todd and I shared the remaining amount and the disagreement quickly dissipated.

Recalling the remainder of the night is like watching your own nightmare; you're trapped and must follow the horrific dream wherever it may take you.

It is only by the grace of God that we didn't kill anyone that night, ourselves included. Our first action, after snorting the speed, was to all jump in a vehicle and go to a bar. The thing about speed is that you are so wired no place you go is comfortable. Everyone is looking at you and so going to a public place is probably the worst thing you can do.

I can barely describe the contradictory feelings of hatred for the high you are on; the crawling suspicion of those around you and yet the fact that for the time being your addiction is being satisfied. You desperately want to climb out of this freak show yet it seems that every time you catch a breath and the high starts to diminish, you immediately replenish it.

It is often said that addiction is a form of insanity. If this horrific cycle doesn't prove this I don't know what would.

Eventually we ran out of the drug and sixteen hours later we all started to come down. Of course we had jobs so we tried to go home and get some sleep. After ingesting speed, people do not sleep for a very long time.

After tossing and turning in my bed, with dark and half remembered memories haunting me, I finally had to go to work. I had not slept in about three days and had topped off this latest binge with an evening of crank.

Try as I might to work effectively, I was simply kidding myself that I was functioning properly. I spent the day falling asleep while trying to talk to customers on the phone. I would answer a call and wake up some time later with no remembrance of picking up the phone.

The day only got worse from there. At the time I had no more drugs, and therefore couldn't sustain myself through the day in my usual fashion. I had an appointment to try and convince the owner of a twenty five unit apartment building to allow us to manage his property.

You must remember I was from a far less hot climate and after seven or eight months living in California I was still not acclimatized to the heat. So when the owner of the property asked that I join him on the roof and discuss our proposal, it didn't take long before the damage I was doing to my body, the residual effects of the night before and the fact I was still unaccustomed to the temperature caused the world to start to spin.

Before passing out on the roof of this building, my last memory is that of a horrified look on the property owner's face. Later he told me I had literally changed color twice in front of him, turning from a sickly pale white to grey. My eyes rolled back in my head and I went down.

Once again I was saved from myself, as luckily I wasn't standing close to the edge of the building. Had I been, I would have surely died. Needless to say we didn't obtain the contract with this gentleman no matter how much I later tried to convince him it was simply due to the heat. I believe he knew different.

As happens with the vast majority of those lost in their addiction, things went from bad to worse. I have never heard of anyone saying that as their disease progressed, things improved.

The night that I hit bottom one of our group members, Jeff, had received a fairly sizeable amount of money. Although I do not recall where he got the funds it was ultimately unimportant and after a quick call the deal was set up.

Jeff and I drove to Alameda County. Unbeknownst to both Jeff and me, Alameda has a very strict policy on drugs and the prison sentences are significant. Truthfully though, had we known it certainly wouldn't have stopped us from going there to purchase the drugs.

Like straight out of the movies, or so I thought, we met with my dealer in a dark parking lot. Jeff leaned out of his window and the transaction was made. Both cars quickly left the area and we headed back to the apartment.

Although we had previously decided we would wait until we got back to the apartment to use the drugs, we were addicts and there was little chance we would be able to hold out the twenty minutes it would take us to get to a safer place.

Predictably it wasn't long before we were parked on a residential street, oblivious to the people in their houses and the chances we would get caught. As I said, when you're lost in your addiction nothing else matters, especially when you're about to satisfy that crawling, all consuming need to replenish your high.

As we sat and talked Jeff handed me a gram of cocaine for driving him to the meet. One can tell from this that he had obtained a lot because it is not often that drug abusers share what they have. I quickly stuffed the gram into my coat pocket and eyed the line of cocaine that Jeff was cutting up.

I honestly do not know how long we remained there doing lines and thinking we were on top of the world before there was a knock on my window. Looking up I saw a police officer tapping my window with his flashlight.

Everything stopped. I felt like I was frozen in time. My heart seemed the only thing that was moving and it was racing now at a dangerous pace. At that exact moment, as I stared into the police officer's face, I knew my nightmare was just beginning.

Just prior to the cop's arrival, Jeff and I had decided our buzz was sufficient and were going to head home. We had cleaned up the mess and Jeff had his baggie under his leg. Whispering to Jeff to stuff the bag under the seat, I turned to try and block the view of the cop as I rolled down the window.

After a few preliminary questions I was asked to step out of the car. I am sure that my condition and the fact I was under the influence of one drug or another was apparent. Stepping out of the car felt like moving through mud. The adrenalin had kicked in to such a high level that it felt like every one of my nerves was standing on end.

Meanwhile a second officer approached Jeff's side of the car and began questioning him. Apparently someone in the neighborhood had called and complained about this suspicious car sitting on their street.

The officer escorted me several feet away from the car and began asking the standard questions like "What are you doing here?" "Where have you been tonight?" and "Where are you going?" I found myself transitioning into my normal demeanor for these types of situations. I often think now that if I hadn't normally been so slick when dealing with the police in the past perhaps I would have hit bottom sooner.

After presenting my Canadian driver's license to the officer, I was soon engaged in a conversation about where I was from. The policeman soon began telling me stories of how he had traveled there and how much he had enjoyed that particular vacation.

It was at this point that I heard the second officer questioning Jeff and things were not going anywhere near as well.

"Where are you going tonight?" the officer inquired. "To my girlfriend's house" Jeff replied and from there it all went downhill. Jeff was obviously nervous and anyone within a hundred meters could probably tell he was trying to hide something.

The officer asked "What street does your girlfriend live on?" Jeff couldn't think of a name since we were not familiar with the area. "What is your girlfriend's first and last name?" the cop asked, Jeff floundered for a bit before coming up with the name Angela. He then told the officer "I don't know her last name."

I remember thinking, as I stood there half listening to the officer regale me with stories of travel experiences, how idiotic Jeff's answers were and wondering just how much longer this was going to go on before the inevitable arrest.

As it turned out, it wasn't very long at all. The officer with Jeff asked him to step out of the car. Apparently Jeff had tried to stuff the bag in between the bottom and top portions of the seat and had failed miserably. As Jeff stepped out, the bag was in plain view.

"I hope this is not marijuana" the officer said. Nope I thought it sure isn't! The officer pulled out the baggie which contained about 10 grams of individually packaged cocaine. "Wow" he said "This doesn't look like marijuana to me."

The cop beside me made a quick transition from small talk to action and I found myself in his grasp. Immediately his hands were searching through my coat and ultimately came across the gram I had previously pocketed.

"What's this?" he asked and even at a time like this I was trying to play the smart ass and replied "marijuana?"

Both Jeff and I were placed under arrest. We stood on the side of the street as the police called for backup including a dog to sniff for more drugs.

Placed in individual cars so we couldn't get our stories straight, we watched as the dog climbed through the car in search of more drugs. During this time I got the bright idea to remove the piece of paper with my dealers name and number on it from my back pocket and stuff it between the seats. An even more difficult operation when one is handcuffed.

One of the officers must have seen my actions and before we left for the police station, I was asked to get out of the car. He quickly lifted up the seat to find the piece of paper lying there. It is odd the thoughts that come to one's head at a time like this. I remember thinking with contempt "Well at least I was able to stuff the paper all the way under the seat, unlike Jeff and his handicapped efforts."

It wasn't long before we were transported to the Oakland jail. We were separated, fingerprinted and photographed. If this was a movie I certainly wasn't enjoying it and I found myself wondering how I could give up my part in this apparent tragedy.

As I stood there, still in shock at everything that had transpired to this point, I remember wondering just how bad was this going to get.

The horrific answer to that question was soon revealed.

Chapter 9

"California Ash"

As the shock started to wear off the true depth of the problems I was facing, having just been arrested and now in jail, were slowly starting to sink in.

Jail is by nature a dismal, desperate place. Some do not believe in such things as negative energy but I bet those people have never been in a jail. The years of broken dreams, lunacy and violence cling to the walls like mold. The air is thick with oppression that weighs down on you.

When you first enter a cell you are immediately hit by the size of it. The restrictive box seems to instantaneously close around you as the cell door closes. It is almost as if it mocks you "Well tough guy it's just you and me now" as it clangs shut.

After processing, Jeff and I were escorted to separate areas in the jail. I was once again questioned as to the events of the evening and although I stuck to my original answers I wondered what Jeff would say. He had already proven to be less than solid when it came to interrogation.

The police seemed to take a lot of pleasure in describing how much trouble I was in. The fact that I was an illegal immigrant and that having been caught in the same car with that amount of drugs meant I was facing a serious charge.

Since all of the cocaine was in individual packages and due to Alameda's drug polices both Jeff and I had been booked on possession for the purposes of trafficking. As such each of us could be facing up to five years in prison regardless of whether it was our first offence or not.

That is when the cops first broached the idea of perhaps cooperating in exchange for a lesser charge or perhaps no charge at all. I must admit that although this was an awful situation the act of good cop versus bad cop became apparent. One officer would yell at me for a few minutes until conveniently his partner would calm him down, coming to my aid almost as if he were defending me.

The police finally realized that I wasn't going to be forthcoming with any additional information and so led me to the holding cell where I was allowed to make a phone call. I had never seen a holding cell with a phone in it but I guess this was a night of firsts.

Eventually I was retrieved from the holding cell and put into the general population. A whole new level of fear was reached as I was escorted into an area that held at least fifty other prisoners.

Obviously I kept to myself. There is a fine line in such situations between looking like a target and looking like you're trying to start something. I can honestly say that was one of the worst nights of my life. Everyone slept in the same room. The cots were old, metallic beds and so every time someone moved their bed squeaked.

Every time a bed squeaked I tensed, waiting for someone who had smelled the fresh meat to attack. After a restless night of imagined horrors, dawn came but with it was no release from the nightmare.

When you're a kid and alone at night in your bed you tell yourself that you just have to make it through the night; that as the sun comes up everything will be fine. Unfortunately as you grow older and have to deal with some of the consequences of your actions you come to learn that this is simply a hoax.

A new day doesn't always guarantee a fresh beginning.

The night turned into eternity but like all things this too shall pass and eventually the sun did rise. Excluding no sleep and the constant pressure of having your nerves on end for eight hours, I was unscathed.

There isn't a lot to do in jail beyond living day to day and so when it finally came time for television one hour later that day, it seemed to add some semblance of normalcy to the whole experience.

During the time I was in jail the White House had appointed Clarence Thomas to the Supreme Court and he was undergoing the review committee process. Anita Hill, who had once worked for him, came forth with allegations of sexual misconduct.

I remember thinking as I sat there, that it was all a load of crap and I said out loud "I doubt that. It is probably people that do not want to see a black man on the Supreme Court."

Although I wasn't aware of it, there were several black gang members also watching the news article and they all heard me. I hadn't intended to try and curry favour. It was simply something that slipped out as I watched.

Fortunately for me they were intrigued by my statement, and one of them asked me "Do you really believe that?" I answered "Yes, I didn't fall for all this racism crap but it seemed to me that there would be a lot of powerful white people in the US that would not like a black man on the Supreme Court."

We spoke for a short time. I described Canada as being far less racist than I had found the States and I described how I didn't follow certain racially motivated stereotypes. With that I was in, at least in enough that I was told I didn't have to worry about anything while I was there.

One of the gang members said "I was the token white guy anyway." He was certainly right about that. The number of people of different races in that area of the prison was extraordinary and being white, I was certainly in the minority.

Normally being in a minority would not be a problem for me. However in a place like jail it only takes the smallest difference to separate you from the pack and make you look vulnerable. As such I was appreciative of the protection offered.

By this time I thought I had exhausted all avenues of escaping the situation I was in. No one that I had associated with was willing or able to help. Usually in that type of crowd, once you start to sink, people tend to run for fear you will take them down with you.

As a last ditch effort I contacted one of the property owners I had formed a relationship with and as unlikely as it seemed, he assured me he would help me out.

The next morning I was released on bail after the charges had been filed. The charge was possession with the intent of trafficking. It wasn't enough for the police to pursue a lesser charge of simple possession; they had to go after the maximum.

The property owner, John, came through for me in the end. Here was someone who didn't really know me outside of the business relationship yet was willing to step up and take a chance on someone who had just been arrested for a drug related crime.

Once again it is only in hindsight that I recognize this as yet another helping hand that God extended when I was down.

As I left the jail one of the guards stopped me and suggested; "Maybe you should consider leaving the country."

With no small relief I was released and Alex came to pick me up. The only thing we spoke about on the long ride home was the questions I had been asked and what my answers had been. There was no real sense of empathy or concern about what I had been through. Alex simply wanted to know if I had mentioned his name. After everything he was most concerned about himself.

It was on that ride home that Alex mentioned that he had contacted my parents and that he had informed them that I had been arrested and why.

Imagine my shame when he told me this; and that my parents who had been planning to surprise me with a visit, fearing I was homesick, were now en route to lend aid to their son recently arrested for drugs.

Still shaken I arrived back at the apartment. Alex gave me a stiff drink which I belted down. Even after all I had been through all I wanted was another line of cocaine. I wanted so desperately to simply forget the pain and remove the shame. At the time I didn't realize that those negative feelings would still play such a huge factor fifteen years after the fact.

Alex had to go back to the office and I joined him. On the way I stopped at a telephone booth and made a phone call to my dealer. As covertly as I could I told him what had happened and that the police had his number.

My thinking at the time was that if Jeff ratted the dealer out, I was going to get in front of it, by being up front with him about how much information I had given. Hopefully by telling him that his number was all they had gotten from me he would believe that any additional information must have come from Jeff.

Upon entering the office I was greeted by a call from the company's owner. Trust me this situation was not new to him, he and his company had a long history of shady activity and run-ins with the police.

He told me that the company had to distance themselves from me given my illegal status; and that if questioned I should say I had only been there on a training program. In the interim I was on my own. I was asked to leave the apartment the company was paying for, return the company vehicle and expect no further pay as I was suspended.

Here I was nineteen years old and on my own; soon with no home, no vehicle, no means of support, deserted by those I thought were my friends. I was facing three to five years in jail and I still had to face my parents who were on their way.

I couldn't believe what an awful hand life had dealt me; certainly I was nowhere near as bad as those I had seen in the jail. After all wasn't I above the law? Certainly there could be no consequences for my actions.

Even now it is hard not to look back with disdain at the childish person I was. I was so completely blind to the fact that eventually your actions catch up and it is up to you and only you to deal with that.

This thought process seems so indicative of the addicted. Either we live in denial or we use that which enslaves us to help maintain our blinders.

As soon as the word got out that I had been arrested everyone ran for cover. Turning to those I associated with for help turned out to be as probable as a black man getting help at a KKK rally and so I sat in a cockroach infested hotel and waited for my parents to arrive.

The next day my parents came into town. There was a period of uncomfortable small talk as both sides tried to adjust to the situation I was in. After a while my father said "Okay tell us everything that has gone on and if I find you have lied even once I will turn my back on you." The disappointment in my parent's eyes was all too visible. I could feel their sorrow seeping out of them and filling the room. Facing this almost unbearable guilt I internalized my discomfort and sought a way to feel put upon. It was as if in my mind it was they who were somehow making this situation worse and simply could not understand the difficulties I faced.

Even as I watched the tears slide down my mother's face and the look of dismay on my father's I convinced myself I was the victim; the one who needed unquestioning support and who else better than my parents to clean up my mess. Wasn't it their job after all?

Under the scrutiny of my father's questions I quickly reverted to that which I knew best. I lied. In answer to the question; "How long have you been using cocaine?" I said: "The night I was arrested was the first time I tried it."

Regardless of the consequences of possibly having my father turn his back on me, I still lied.

The remainder of the day was spent with my father and mother investigating my involvement. They commented on the amount of weight I had lost. I continued to stick to my story that the evening of the arrest was my one and only time getting high with cocaine.

One of the people I had associated with was a lawyer. I knew that although he occasionally used drugs he was the best qualified of all of us to offer any real help. The pressure from the police to help them arrest those who had sold us the drugs continued each day. They would call or simply stop by where I was staying.

It finally got to the point where I had my lawyer complain to the judge that the police were endangering my life. The simple fact of the matter was that if my dealer thought for a second I was going to roll on him, I would be dead.

If any of the gang members thought I would rat them out I would be dead.

I spent the next few months trying to hang on. My parents finally had to go back home and left me with some money to try and support myself, I, of course, spent that money on drugs. Trying in vain to once again medicate myself against the intense negative feelings I was experiencing.

Once again my parents had proven their love for me, standing behind me and providing great support for which I will always be thankful. I know now that there are many who suffer from addiction who are not as blessed as I too have such an incredible support group.

One of the oddest things I remember from that time was being taken out for lunch by the president of the company I was working for. During lunch he told me "The only thing you did wrong was getting caught." I was stunned. I had thought perhaps getting involved in drugs was the problem; but apparently had I not been caught I would have been innocent.

I saw Todd only once after that. He came by the fleabag hotel I was staying at and started asking odd questions about myself and some of the people we did business with. To this day I am convinced he was working with the police to either get my charges increased or implicate others to have his charges reduced.

I knew that all I had to do was make one phone call and Todd would disappear. No one would take the chance that he might work a deal with the police. Knowing that I so easily have someone's life ended seemed repulsive and yet intoxicating.

For fear that anyone I called may decide to include my death in the solution they came up with convinced me not to call.

I won't lie. There were many times when helping the police in exchange for a removal of the charges seemed attractive; but at the end of the day if someone ratted it wasn't going to me. I would take my lumps but at least I wouldn't have to look over my shoulder all the time, looking for someone getting ready to put two in the back of my head.

My lawyer continued to work on my case behind the scenes and finally negotiated a plea of guilty for the lesser charge of possession if I would agree to leave the country and not be allowed to return to California for two years.

Even at the airport I was escorted to the gate by city police.

With my tail tucked between my legs I boarded a flight back to Vancouver BC Canada; where I would be the assistant manager of the same company that just a few weeks ago had left me high and dry.

In Vancouver I would initially move into my dad's apartment. He was there working on a contract for a methanol company.

I had gone to California with a chance to really accomplish something. Through my addiction and through the choices I made I gave up that dream.

I have often heard people said that those things they no longer have because of their addiction, they lost. To me one must stand up and be accountable for their actions. I did not lose my dreams. I did not have my chances taken away from me. I forfeited them all for drugs.

The day I left for Vancouver was the day the wildfires of California were in full swing. I awoke, looked outside and it appeared like it was snowing, so intensely was the ash falling in the parking lot.

Even at the time I didn't think there could be a better symbol for my time in California. The usually bright and warm sun covered by the ashes of the dreams that I once held for my coming to this area. As the ashes continued to fall I couldn't help making the same comparison to what I perceived would be the rest of my life.

Of all the people I had spent time with in Oakland no one followed up with me as to how I was transitioning. No one sent a card with good wishes. To this day the only person I have even heard anything about was Alex. Apparently he went to Hawaii, got into a bad crowd and disappeared.

I had hit bottom. This must be the end of the fall, right? Like a lot of addicts I found a trapdoor to my bottom and the fall continued.

In spite of all that I had been through I still had more to learn and a lot farther down to fall.

Chapter 10

"The Walking Dead: An Introspective"

Leaving California was both a release of months of tension and yet also a letdown. It was as if even in this most desperate of situations I had once again stumbled onto a life that allowed me to revel in danger and feed my substance addiction I had spent time with gangs, faced death and spent time in jail, yet there was a very large part of me that soon missed California as soon as I had left it. As I have often said part of the addiction, for me, was the life; throwing myself into situations that when I survived proved I was invincible and fearless. Little did I know that it would be years before I understood the meaning of the word courage.

Moving to Vancouver allowed me time to repair the damage I had done in California. It offered me a chance to mend fences and rebuild bridges that I had destroyed. The main problem was that I was still active in my addiction and so at the time, this opportunity didn't seem as clear as it does now.

Soon I was back at work with the same company that had so quickly walked away from me in California. I tried to justify this at the time by telling myself that I would have done the same and that given the lifestyle I was living I should expect no less.

However, deep inside I felt a great sense of abandonment. Real or imagined, those feelings became a part of my reality. My inability to trust was reinforced and so having decided long ago I was in this world alone I continued on, a prisoner of my own perceptions.

When considering the effects of withdrawal my first day back was the most difficult. I was unaccustomed to the city and so cruising around looking for drugs did not seem plausible; not to mention the fact that at the time I had been out of work for a while and therefore had no money.

As I sat there trying to drown out the cravings by watching television I wrestled with the crawling, desperate need for dope. Soon it became an all-consuming sensation. I grew sick to my stomach and broke out into a sweat. I felt both lethargic and restless all at the same time. Minutes turned into hours as I tried to ignore the demons that were plaguing me.

Even in recollection I cannot remember that day ending! It is as if I saw that time frame as an eternity and still I cannot fathom that the pain ever in fact stopped.

Soon I was back at work, trying to fit in with a new group. Given my experiences I fell back on a demeanor of bullying, sarcasm and attempted domination. How obvious it was to others that the behavior denoted an overwhelming feeling of insecurity and an inability to deal with normal social situations I don't know.

As time went by, I climbed the corporate ladder. I also made connections outside of the office that fulfilled the need to satisfy my addictions. Having promised myself that I would not go near hard drugs again I justified the usage of marijuana. After all, this was British Columbia, where the vast majority of Canada's pot is grown. I felt as if I were finally part of society as a whole, as so many others used marijuana.

Once again each new day seemed to be an unpleasant yet necessary step I had to take so that I could make it to the evening where I would be able to smoke myself into oblivion. Marijuana is substantially cheaper than cocaine and so I was able to consume much more. Even so, the vast majority of the money I was earning soon was directed at obtaining the drug.

It was not long before marijuana was not enough to feed the beast within; yet again the voices of insecurity and perceived boredom became too loud. I soon added alcohol to my nightly ritual. I would arrive home having purchased a new six pack of beer. I would roll a joint and then as quickly as possible consume all the beer while killing additional brain cells with the pot.

I would continue using each night until I finally passed out. All too soon the morning would come and I would start the routine all over. The pattern of dragging through the day and feeding my addiction at night became constant. In retrospect I do not know how many years I wasted as I closed my eyes to reality and withdrew into my self-created world of sleeping through life.

It was not long before I attracted into this routine those that were also sick and soon there was a group of us. Each member assuring the other as to how "with it" they were by duplicating the others actions and attitudes. Some of the people in this group were from work but most were from outside of that environment.

That way I could once again start to dip my toe into another world, one that included danger and fed the other part of my addiction. Soon our evenings were no longer filled with slowly killing ourselves alone. As we each took our accumulated emotional baggage and visited our perceptions of reality on others, we became increasingly more active in the social circles we had formed.

Quickly I progressed from associating with minor drug dealers and those that acted as I did and graduated into a class of bikers and drug dealers.

To this day it strikes me as to how blind I had become to the reality that my actions and attitudes were not of the norm. Having surrounded myself with likeminded people I was able to delude myself with justification and self-centered behavior, not once questioning whether there was something better.

Long before my time in Vancouver I had resigned myself to the perception that a life of searching for and consuming drugs was all there was. Any activity outside of that pursuit was only completed if it enabled me to satisfy the need for narcotics and the lifestyle that accompanies them.

I worked because I needed to earn money to support my habit. I got involved in romantic relationships only if the other person could be manipulated into providing my emotional requirements. Only if she was able to justify my feelings of self-pity and self-centeredness would the relationship continue.

It was during my time in Vancouver that I met and fell in love with Lisa. It would not be for many years after the breakup of our five year relationship that I would realize that at that point in my life I had no real concept of love.

We met when I answered an ad for a roommate. Although she was involved in a relationship, it was not long before I started to subtly manipulate conversations towards the goal of stealing her away from her boyfriend.

It was near the end of their relationship that the three of us went out for dinner. I, of course, was stoned and had plenty to drink during the meal. As such, my memory of the following events is hazy at best.

I remember climbing into the backseat of her boyfriend's car after dinner as we prepared to go home. The restaurant was located on the opposite side of Hastings Street in Burnaby, a suburb of Vancouver. We had four lanes of extremely heavy traffic to cross not to mention the fact that it had been raining, and so traction was poor.

I recall the car spinning out as Lisa's boyfriend gunned the engine. I had been setting my leftovers on the seat beside me when I happened to look up and see a pair of headlights. I distinctly remember the phrase "Oh shit" running through my head and then I lost consciousness.

The next thing I remember was Lisa asking me if I was alright. I replied that I was and started to scratch an itch on my forehead. It wasn't until I looked at my hand that I noticed that it was covered in blood. I once again passed out.

I awoke to find the fireman removing me from the car and putting me on a stretcher. I remember being so incredibly angry that a crowd had gathered, not unlike vultures, to witness the carnage.

To this day I often wonder how many were dissatisfied with our show since no one had died.

In addition to the numerous stitches it required to sew up the gash in my head, leaving a scar still visible on my forehead today, I also separated both shoulders. Perhaps I should have put on my seat belt?

The most significant part of my involvement in the car accident is the fact that it served as my introduction to prescription pills. I was sent home the same evening of the car wreck, a bottle of Tylenol 3 with codeine in my hand.

It is as clear as yesterday to me, recalling the sensation I felt as the medication took effect. I reveled in the release of my pain, both physical and mental. I soon grew accustomed to the warming feeling as the drugs kicked in.

Here was the answer to my prayers. I had come across a drug that provided everything that I wanted from its consumption and yet it was legal and not frowned upon by society. In fact here was a tool that subverted my emotions and made my consumption of it easy to defend.

After all I had been in an accident! Later as my need for more drugs continued, I fell back on my history of migraines. When that stopped working I would create pains, sometimes real, sometimes imagined, and run off to the doctor to get more relief.

Although my drinking during this time became less frequent, trips to the bar with those I worked with were frequent and never short. We would often drink ourselves into oblivion; getting into all the trouble that involves, such as 24 hour suspensions for driving while intoxicated or bar fights.

Our drinking soon became well known and the bars we would frequent would often reserve a table for us each and every night. One night we would spend at a disreputable strip club filled with patrons and prostitutes and the next at a well-known dance club. In each bar we were greeted warmly, offered free drinks and would often stay well past closing, drinking with the owners and staff of the establishment.

What no one knew at the time was that I would be accenting my buzz with whatever the pill of the week was. Many of us would often slip outside to partake in a joint. There are so many nights that I will never be able to recall beyond leaving for the evening and then taking whatever substance I could, be it pills, liquor or marijuana to the point of no memory.

Like alcohol, my marijuana usage decreased as my pill consumption increased. I worked my way from Tylenol 3's through almost any kind of sleeping pill I could find to morphine and Demerol; anything that would dull my pain and blind me to life.

There were times when I was unable to procure a refill without alerting people to my addiction. In these periods I would simply go to a local drugstore and purchase Tylenol 1's that still had codeine in them. Of course I felt totally justified in consuming 10 – 12 pills at a time.

During these times it was not uncommon for me to go through a bottle of one hundred tablets in less than two days. As such when it came time to refill the prescription for the "better" drugs, I could justify it by telling myself that at least I wasn't consuming so much of the lesser pills.

That is really all my life was about for approximately four years. I can recall moments where I even started to recognize the potential that maybe I had a problem and even once entered a detox center. Needless to say I felt persecuted by the hand life had dealt me and soon left long before I came to realize the miracles that are available in recovery.

My perception at the time as I watched my life crumble around me was that I had been dealt a bad hand. Perhaps I was an addict, but what could anyone expect from me? After all if you had to endure the daily routine of boredom and perceived persecution that I did, you would turn to drugs as well.

I was blessed at the time to have a few true friends that wanted nothing more from me than my happiness and a return of those wishes for themselves. They sought nothing from me other than respect and camaraderie. Unfortunately I was too self-involved to realize the strength one can get from a relationship like that.

One of these friendships was with a guy named Bruce. We met while playing hockey and had quickly formed a friendship that extended outside of the rink. We began spending more and more time together and I quickly found out that Bruce was someone who didn't care about the little pieces of my history that I shared nor judged me for my obvious drug usage.

Although Bruce refrained from drugs we would often go out drinking in a large group. Bruce's drinking never seemed to be as a result of a need. There were, of course, evenings that in a drunken state we each became involved in events that were to our and others detriment, such as drinking and driving or getting into scrapes with other intoxicated patrons, but I never once saw Bruce's drinking as paralleling my own.

Whether I knew it at the time I was aware, on some level, that while Bruce could move on in life leaving the drink behind I was enslaved to it and the other vices I chased.

The depths of Bruce's friendship were not realized until many years later when I finally hit the bottom of my bottoms. Through the hell that ensued Bruce stuck with me. As I write this now Bruce is still my closest and most trusted friend. In fact, it is safe to say he is the only friend from those days who is still by my side.

Without fail, my relationship with Lisa soon disintegrated and although we stuck together, even threw a move to Alberta; I believe we each knew our days together were numbered.

As with my life at the time I felt far more comfortable with the devil I knew. As such, being involved in a negative relationship was easier and somehow felt appropriate. On some level ensuring that I was in a sick relationship allowed me to keep myself from feeling happy, an emotion that was both foreign and felt undeserved.

After many years of working with the property management company, regardless of the achievable goals and financial freedom I was nearing, I left the company. I can now see that once again I had come too close to a feeling of security and happiness and had found a way to sabotage it.

After many months of pretending to find work and instead filling my days with the pursuit and usage of any substance I could get my hands on, Lisa and I decided to move to Calgary, Alberta.

Although the move seemed logical at the time, I can now see it for what it was; an attempt to escape from the emotional and financial hole we had dug. The problem, as they say when you move under these circumstances, is that you take yourself with you.

My problems followed me to Calgary and soon I was on a path that would certainly lead to my death, barring a miracle.

Unbeknownst to me at the time my bottom was fast approaching and the pain and hell I was going to experience in Calgary was like nothing I had ever been through. The time in jail and the time spent in California were tame when compared to what lay in wait for me.

Chapter 11

"Defenseless"

As with all geographical escape attempts, my move to Calgary proved unsuccessful in correcting the path I was on. Although Lisa and I stumbled through another year of a failed relationship the end was inevitable.

Soon I found myself alone. Lisa was gone and I had already managed to distance myself from my family. Most of the people I used to associate with had either died or were incarcerated.

Oddly enough there were still a few from the original group that had managed to hang on and so I found myself spending more time with them.

Given the alternative of having to face the negative emotions my lifestyle was providing or increase my drug use I chose the latter. As with my time in Vancouver my life was spent in an effort to simply pass time. Opportunities to excel or to improve myself were passed up in favour of the all too comfortable feeling of darkness.

Such emotions as happiness, a sense of growth and serenity seemed foreign, unreliable and most importantly undeserved.

It is only now when looking back that I can comprehend the true depths of the hole I had dug for myself. My daily rituals consisted of nothing more than perpetuating my feelings of despair and loneliness.

After Lisa's departure from my life, I quickly tail spun into a pattern of emotional self-abuse and increased drug usage.

Unfortunately at the time I did not seem aware that the choices that had led me down this path were my own and as such I was the person that needed to deal with the consequences of my actions. Constantly blaming others and life for my predicament only served to keep me chained.

It is a sad thing to look back at portions of your life and to realize that during that time your contribution to society or more importantly to yourself was negligible at best. I, of course, did not think I had a problem with drugs or a problem confronting my emotions.

To me the daily routine of sleepwalking through life was the norm; after all how could anyone who had been dealt the hand I had expect better?

At this time in my life I was still what was considered a "functioning addict." To most I was an active member of society. Through my eldest brother I soon landed a job working in telecommunications and I proceeded to become successful in this industry.

My outward appearance was that of an up and comer, accepting and accomplishing the tasks that would lead towards a successful path. This apparent success in my new career and the supposed ability to overcome the difficulties I have faced in my life started to become a source of pride for those around me.

My family, as always, was supportive of my accomplishments and often took the time to tell me how proud they were.

To me these were words of poison. Can you imagine a mind that is more comfortable with feelings of pain and despair than those of acceptance or happiness? New found success and accomplishment was so completely uncomfortable to me that quickly I found ways to sabotage them.

Perhaps you, the reader, view these statements as overly self-effacing or even whiny but it is only through my new found ability to confront the truth of these emotions, my actions to sabotage success and an overwhelming feeling of unworthiness that I can finally confront the reality of that mind set.

Only through this self-examination and the realization of the part I played in those situations can I learn and grow. It is not my intent to ridicule myself for past misdeeds nor do I feel the need to wallow in those actions but rather to face the past, cleanse myself from its hold on me and come to the final determination that it is what it is.

The actions, misdeeds and negative perceptions of the past are something I can now distinguish from the path I am on currently. The past is just that, the past.

I wound up working in telecommunications for almost seven years. Through this time it was a constant up and down of emotions, success and failure. I was successful and wound up earning a reputable income; quickly I became a respected member of my peer group in the industry and enjoyed the financial rewards that came.

After Lisa's and my relationship fell apart I convinced myself that once again I had been dealt a poor hand. I was destined to never have a meaningful relationship. Once again I believed I was placed upon this earth to suffer and another failed relationship only served to enforce this misconception.

It was not in my nature at the time to examine my role in the failure of our relationship. It was far more comfortable to believe that I was born to suffer and simply had to accept that strife was all I could expect from life.

After Lisa all other romantic relationships were short lived at best. Girlfriend, after girlfriend, was cast aside as soon as they became too close. I found almost comical reasons to ensure a break up.

In no way was I going to allow myself to become close to another, this only led to pain. My belief at the time was that an end to a relationship was destined from the moment that the relationship began. Only now can I see that it was mostly through my actions and inability to trust in another that the relationship's end was inevitable.

I was a loner, and all of my energy and actions were directed towards maintaining that loneliness.

This belief soon found its way into my relationship with my family. So completely uncomfortable was I with acceptance that I simply could not trust them. I truly believed that if they knew me and the secrets of my past there was no way their acceptance would continue.

Contrary to all that my family had done to demonstrate an attitude of forgiveness and acceptance, I felt that once they found out my true nature they would cast me aside, repulsed by the perpetrator of falsehood in their midst.

As usual when confronted with success and happiness I turned to drugs. My consumption of drugs increased. It did not take long for me to begin "Doctor shopping" and soon I had found a good resource of doctors that I could convince of my problems. From migraines to accidents I was able to continuously increase my list of those who would provide me with what I needed to medicate against my emotional pain.

Evenings were filled with drinking and using marijuana. Difficulties with my kidneys and liver started to increase in direct correlation with the ever increasing amount of pills and alcohol.

I even came to the point where sleep was impossible without downing a six pack of beer, a couple of sleeping pills and smoking several joints. I would wake up in the morning and my first thought was getting to the stash of pills, usually something with codeine, which would clear the fog of the night before.

On and on my days were filled with three to four hour segments as I watched the clock waiting for the next acceptable time to down more pills. Often I wouldn't be able to wait and the four hour period slowly reduced to three hours, than two and so on.

Often I would have to leave work early due to the fact I had made myself sick from my intake of the medication. I would return home and simply get an early start on the usage of some of the other drugs in my arsenal.

I was quickly digging a hole for myself that would be impossible to climb out of without the help of others. Only now have I come to understand the true difficulty in finding someone to help when you do not trust anyone. When you feel truly destined to wallow in the mire of self-depreciation and self-destruction turning to others is a truly foreign concept; after all this is what life was all about. The only problem I thought I had with drugs was ensuring I had enough.

This is the point in my life when I was first truly exposed to the usage of needles for the delivery of drugs. I had gotten so good at convincing the many doctors I visited of the severity of whatever ailment was currently using to solicit drugs that I was offered more immediate cures through injections.

It was not long before I would visit doctors day after day to receive an ever increasing dosage of Demerol. Seventy five milligrams a dose slowly was increased to double that size. I was constantly impressed by the effectiveness of this method of delivering the drugs. Within seconds of the injection I would start feeling the comforting sensations of warmth and tranquility.

Being so completely under the control of the dosage I would often find myself at home lost in space, eyes glued to the television and only then realizing that I had gotten a shot, rented movies and was wasting the day away in front of the idiot box and that I had in fact driven home in this condition.

Even the realization of how lucky I was to be alive and not to have killed anyone while driving home did nothing to deter me as I went to the doctors the next time.

I wonder now how much time was spent in a doctor's office awaiting my next release. If the doctor became suspicious and refused to give me either the prescription I wanted or the injection I thought I needed, I would simply go to another medical clinic and start the procedure over.

At that point doctors and medical staff were not there to help the injured or truly sick, they were there to fill my ever increasing need for drugs. After a while I stopped caring what drugs were provided just so long as they provided that sensation of release.

The worst times were those when I found myself without any medication. The act of consuming handfuls of Tylenol #1's was no longer sufficient and my body had begun to fight back against this poison. Severe heartburn, digestive problems, significant weight loss and general poor health were not enough to convince me I had to choose a better path.

It is hard to describe the true nature of withdrawal. The sweating and physical pain, the nightmares and shakes were only the beginning when compared to the sickening need and the desperation for more drugs that one experiences. If hell were to truly be on earth, I imagine it would be much like these sensations.

The depravity of the disease is demonstrated through the fact that no matter how far down I slid, regardless of the dangers of usage or the horrors of withdrawal, I never thought twice when the opportunity to consume more drugs presented itself again.

To this day it still amazes and sickens me how through this downward spiral I was able to maintain an appearance of normalcy. To the outsider I appeared as a normal person, a responsible member of society, when in fact inwards I was killing myself.

Now I can see that through this entire time I was trying to commit suicide. So ever present was the pain of my life thus far, the guilt and shame over my past and the feeling of unworthiness to anything better, that I had subconsciously decided that life was not worth living.

Happiness and hope were emotions for the blessed; for those that had somehow curried the favor of God and were for some reason destined to live better than I. I had given up without really trying. I had resigned myself to death and now I was trying to ensure that seemingly inevitable end.

I now believe that other than the miracles provided by God that it is only due to the fact I hadn't the nerve to use a gun that I am here to speak of this. That it is only through the fact that I had chosen a slow end rather than a quick conclusion am I alive today.

Feelings of utter hopelessness and despair were so comfortable and easy for me to accept that I in fact attempted to drag out the final conclusion. Before the inevitable end I attempted to make the most of my time wallowing in my negative emotions and situation.

As such I approached the bottom of all bottoms. I was not prepared for the pain I would endure or the pain I would visit upon those around me.

Considering my emotional state, the dependence on drugs and my inability to trust others I was completely unprepared for the inevitable end that was fast approaching.

Chapter 12

"Responsibility Comes Second"

Addiction by nature seems to be an ongoing example of insanity. As an addict I continued to surround myself with situations that would reinforce my negative outlook on all aspects of my life. My relationships were tainted by my constant manipulation and my need to ensure that everyone around me was fully aware of the emotional defects I carried.

My career was constantly under siege by the overriding need to satisfy my addiction, days were cut short as I left to go find a doctor to provide the injection I was searching for. Even when I was physically at work I was mentally absent since I was usually under the influence of one narcotic or another.

Such is addiction, a disease that snakes its way into all aspects of your life. Like a cancer it slowly rots you from the inside out and soon controls all. Addiction is a clever disease. While it spreads its taint it convinces you that your downward slide is normal.

The vast majority of my time back in Calgary was nothing more than an exercise in killing time. Whether you are aware of it or not, while you are killing time, you are slowly killing yourself.

Since moving back to Calgary I passed the time by ensuring my needs were filled. All my attention was paid to the self-serving need to feed my addiction. The disease required that I not only provide a chemical solution but that I also revel in the negative emotions one experiences in life as an addict.

It is only now that I am realizing that if I am to have a disease at least it is addiction. I can now honestly say I feel blessed that if I were to have a disease at least I have one that can be treated at least the affects can be monitored and controlled.

After years of feeding my addiction I met Susan. We dated on and off and endured a very rocky relationship, yet when the time came to consider marriage both of us jumped in. Regardless of the fact we had only known each other a very short time and that our relationship to date had been troublesome, I believe we both turned to marriage since we mistakenly thought this would be the answer to all of our problems.

I believe that sick people attract sick people and with that in mind it should be no surprise that both Susan and I were sick in our own ways. Each of us carried our own baggage into our marriage and it was not long before that baggage worked its way into every aspect of our relationship.

Although I do not believe either of us were aware of it at the time, I think we each jumped at a marriage with the thought process that it would fix us of all that ailed us. We were both far too self-centered to understand the work that was required to provide a loving and healthy environment for our partner.

It is difficult to maintain a relationship when each person is far more interested in satisfying their individual wants and desires. Attempting to fix these types of problems through the act of getting married is like trying to use gasoline to put out a fire.

Regardless of the fact that my constant search and use of prescription medication was becoming more evident and that I had continued to drink and often topped up my buzz with marijuana I still somehow maintained a career and in fact continued to succeed.

I earned a decent income and soon was caught up in the trappings of money. It was not long before an obsession for possessions took over. I had to have the best and most expensive vehicle, the nicest clothes and I would often throw money around in a vain attempt to prove how great I was: simply because I had money.

Most of it was an illusion. My credit cards soon were close to their limit and the monthly bills became an ever increasing encumbrance on my goal of living the high life. The thought process of truly believing you are owed this type of lifestyle and should be able to carry it out regardless of your true financial position seems to me to be just another indication of the insanity found in addiction. I had reached the point where the drugs I was taking were not meeting my ever increasing need to satisfy the hole I felt in life, as such I turned to the trappings of monetary gain and consumerism.

I have always been one who enjoyed the innocence that children have. I can honestly say that I tend to relate to children far more easily than I do adults and so it was not long before Susan became pregnant and we both eagerly awaited the birth of our first child.

In the face of this approaching miracle one might think that I was presented with not only the opportunity but the motivation to clean up my lifestyle and finally take into consideration the needs of another.

This, unfortunately, was not the case. My desire to have a child was in itself almost entirely yet another personification of the self-centeredness I had immersed myself in. I continued to use prescription medication as often as possible and would usually have a large quantity of pain meds and sleeping pills at hand.

My trips to the doctor became ever more regular and it was not long before it became a daily routine to end up at a doctor's office in search of the medication that would quiet the voices of insecurity and the demons of my addiction. Emotion and the ability to live a productive life were equally suppressed.

It is impossible for me to recall this part of my life without tears! Even now, years later, the guilt of how I put myself ahead of this young life and how my addiction always superseded his needs haunts me in my dreams and in my waking hours.

Susan did not have an easy pregnancy. She developed a reaction that caused severe rash and itching. The child was in breach and to top it off, shortly before the birth of our son Susan injured her ribs getting out of our SUV. This combination meant that she wound up enduring a very painful pregnancy.

Even through all of her troubles in carrying our son, my needs and desires came first. The ever present crawling desire to feed my addiction was first and foremost.

Susan eventually had to be hospitalized due to the pain she was experiencing. Within a day or so the doctors decided that due to the position of our son in her womb and the difficulties with her ribs that they would perform a C section.

Within hours our son was born. I held this innocent child in my arms and looked into the eyes of unconditional love, of true acceptance and the need for protection.

God had blessed me with the birth of a healthy boy and in the face of this miracle my true feelings were centered on myself because as I stood there with the proof of God's love in my arms I was high on Demerol.

My son's first experience with the man that had been charged with the responsibility of providing his emotional and physical needs, with the man who had accepted the role of his guide in life, was being held by him while he was under the influence of a narcotic.

The richness of the moment, the witnessing of the miracle, the pure love and serenity had all been forfeited for self-fulfillment and a desire to stuff my emotions by whatever means possible.

My son is my inspiration! He is by far the greatest gift ever given to me and is the object of my unconditional love. Imagine the crawling feelings of guilt and remorse that still haunt me as I recognize the fact that when offered a chance to witness his birth I chose to do so while intoxicated.

There are so many aspects of the disease addiction that can affect areas such as these. There is the selfishness, the ever present need to feed your addiction, the self-pity and perhaps worst of all the feeling you are not worthy of the happiness represented through the birth of a child.

Soon our sons came home, and try as best as we could, we were unable to truly give him the attention he needed because it was at this time I was reintroduced to cocaine. Only this time it came in the form of crack.

It was a few months after our son was born that we held a New Year's Eve party. It was, after all, not only New Year's but also my birthday, so there was reason for celebration. A friend who was attending the party took me downstairs and offered me a chance to smoke something he had brought.

Although at the time I had heard of crack I had never used it and had never seen it close up. The release of the intoxicating effect was immediate, my head spun and my ears rung as it took effect.

It is a natural progression for an addict to gravitate towards harder drugs. Simply put, I strongly believe that those who smoke marijuana and do not believe the potential that it has to be in fact a stepping stone drug are simply fooling themselves and are truly ignorant of the potential path that lies in wait for them.

With the first inhale of the smoke produced by the crack I was hooked. Much like when I first experienced cocaine, I was immediately taken by the effectiveness of the drug. In my mind I was separated from the ongoing difficulties I found in life and thus I felt delivered.

Within weeks the need for crack became more and more pressing. There were times I recognized the dangerous path I was on and even tried to quit; however reinforced by Susan's acceptance and usage of the drug, I continued on.

Our son took a back seat to our using, luckily I have a loving family who would take our son and look after him. I would tell them anything I could to justify the ever increasing amount of time he spent at their home; whether it was a fight Susan and I were having or neither of us feeling well, the lies were plentiful.

Even when he was at home with us we could barely wait for him to go to bed. Somehow we justified our using by doing it at night when he was asleep. The fact that as a baby he would wake often and the ever present chance he may need more attention than a quick hug never seemed to be a concern when faced with a chance to use.

The first year of my son's life is hard to envision. The cloudiness that formed in my mind as a result of so completely immersing myself into the life of an active addict prevents me from recalling this time clearly.

It was not long before it became difficult to support the habit financially; obviously my effectiveness at work decreased and my days were once again filled with satisfying my need to quiet the monkey on my back.

So when the opportunity to sell drugs came along and I realized I could use this to provide the means to support my own personal habit I jumped at it.

Quickly the amount I was selling increased; my phone would constantly ring as addict after addict called to get what they needed. If I came across someone who hadn't used the drug before, it was not uncommon for me to offer a trial piece for free. It was through the act of providing free drugs that I could increase my customer base. I knew that once they tried it and the fact that it was I who had introduced them to it I would be the one they called when the curiosity turned to need.

At the time I didn't care about the path I was leading them down. I never gave a second thought to the fact that I was endangering their lives. Even as I suffered from the effects of addiction I was all too eager to pull people down with me. In the face of this hypocrisy I chose only to focus on the fact that their downfall aided me in maintaining my lifestyle.

The complete separation from what I once held as my belief system is something that still bothers me today.

I thought I had found the key to my survival. I was still earning a decent income through work and was substantially increasing my standard of living via the dealing.

With such a life comes the need to take on the persona of a dealer. Occasionally I would front someone drugs; which is to say I would give them the drug and expect payment later. For those unfortunates that do not pay in time things can get ugly. Harassing phone calls quickly turn into threats of violence and the use of violence when needed.

I have been witness to people being beaten bloody over debts of no more than $10.00. I recall one instance where someone owed an associate $20.00 dollars and when that associate tracked him down he almost beat him to death with a barbell.

That is the life and such situations are not only expected but they are the norm. It is believed that if you are seen to be soft others will take advantage of you. Whether you are trying to protect your "street cred" or you are concerned that someone is trying to steal your customers, violence is always the answer.

This requirement for violence only, of course, breeds more violence and is fueled by addiction. If the only way to ensure you can maintain your lifestyle as an active addict is to physically hurt someone than that is what you do.

By this point I had surrounded myself with hangers-on. Those who only associate with you and build up your ego because you have something they want. They know you have access to drugs and often large quantities and so instantly you become their best friend. If in the end it will accomplish their goal of feeding their addiction these friends will just as soon stick a knife in your back.

It was not long before I spent more and more time away from home. Whether it was in a seedy bar, in the house of someone I didn't really know or simply hanging out with gang members I quickly sank into the life normally associated with addiction.

I turned away from my responsibilities as a friend, as a husband and a father. Worst of all I turned away from my relationship with God and I turned away from myself.

Given my actions and attitudes at the time there was but one direction I could go. Even as I slipped further down I had no real comprehension of how bad things were about to get.

Chapter 13

"A New Master"

My experiences clearly demonstrated to me that once an addict starts heading towards the bottom it comes fast. I had abandoned my family, my friends and myself in search of drugs and the lifestyle that accompanied them.

I can even recall driving while high and feeling sorry for those I saw that were apparently crawling through life straight. "What fools" I thought.

Day by day I sank deeper into self-gratification and self-destruction.

By now I was selling a fairly large quantity of drugs and yet I was beginning to have a problem that even this revenue could not support my ever increasing habit. Soon I began shorting people on the amount I was giving them. Some of the dealers would coat the crack in Visine so that when the customer smoked it; they would automatically pass out; thus leaving them vulnerable to being robbed.

I cannot count the number of times that ideas like this crossed my mind.

My attention to the business of selling drugs soon took a back seat to the using of those drugs. I had broken the cardinal rule of a drug dealer "Never get high on your own supply" and it was not long before all of my time was spent consuming drugs instead of selling them.

I was no longer able to collect on debts, nor did I care. I farmed out the job of collection for a while but even that fell by the wayside as I fell deeper into my own addiction.

I spent an ever increasingly short amount of time at home, regardless of the fact that I had a child at home and a wife. I paid more attention to the pursuit and usage of the drugs I sought.

The type of people I associated with soon declined even more and it would not be unusual for me to be driving around at 2 or 3 am, a car load full of people I had just met. Most of whom would just as soon jack me. All of us in search of drugs.

Prostitutes, drug dealers, pimps and gang bangers became my new family. With these people I found acceptance. I had never felt a part of any group of people before. Even when contemplating the relationship with my family I felt isolated and different.

My family was always supportive yet I felt as if I didn't belong. It was as if they threatened my ability to hide emotion and it was as if I believed that eventually they would find out about my true nature and simply walk away from me.

To me it seemed easier to hide within myself, blanketed by the poison I was using instead of opening myself to any possibility of rejection.

My recollection of these days is difficult. Not only do they still serve as a source of guilt and shame but also given my heavy usage, the memories are often veiled behind a cloud.

Yet through all the depravity of the situations I found myself in I also found that it fed the part of my addiction that liked the chaos. I witnessed or took part in severe beatings, theft and drug deals. I stood by as I watched woman sell their bodies and their souls all in search of that next high.

I was complicit in their downfall because I could not think beyond myself. Their involvement in my life was no more than what I expected to be the norm. Even the violence I saw or took part in, the manipulation, the self-serving actions and attitudes were all considered normal in my sick mind.

It was at this time I received an opportunity to own half of a new company with my father. We had a product that was sure to sell and if marketed properly we could both be very successful with this new endeavor.

I walked away from the telecommunication job I held, due in part to the fact that my ever increasing reliance on drugs began to take its toll on my ability to work and I saw my dismissal as inevitable.

I soon learned that starting a new company and expending the effort to make it work required a lot of determination and hard work. This, of course, impeded my ability to feed my addiction. After months of continuously reduced effort I finally asked my father to buy me out.

I know now that he had started this company with a goal of bringing us closer together; yet here I was having really provided little towards the company's survival, more interested in using drugs, and asking him to give me money to buy my portion of the company.

Reluctantly he agreed and gave me several postdated checks to cover the amount we had agreed upon. Quickly I cashed the first check and used it to procure more drugs. The thoughts of betrayal that is so evident to me now never crossed my mind as I used the proceeds to sink deeper into despair and drug usage.

It did not take long for the funds associated with the first check to run out; by this time my dealing was so limited that it no longer even came close to covering the amount needed to support my habit. It was quite the realization that I could in fact deposit the postdated checks and that the bank would honor them.

Without a second thought to any problems this would cause the company or my father, I cashed the checks and was soon "enjoying" the rush the drugs I had bought with the money provided.

What a clear representation this is of the need to satisfy your addiction; nothing got in the way of my using. Even though I knew I was betraying my father's trust and jeopardizing his future by taking these funds from the company sooner than I had agreed to, it meant nothing to me at the time.

I was high and nothing else mattered.

Now I would sometimes be away from my home for days. The dependence my child had on me was only an inconvenient encumbrance to the lifestyle I was trying to lead. My nights and soon even my days were spent downtown or hanging out with fellow users. Even the circle of people I used to associate with in my business as a dealer, began to know me as another strung out junkie. No longer was I calling them to restock for my customers but now it was me phoning at all hours of the day to buy drugs for my own personal use.

I had gone from being the supplier to yet another user and not for one second did any of them hesitate in giving me what I wanted. The only prerequisite was money. So long as I had that they were my best friend and would gladly hand over the poison that I was killing myself with. Just as I had done in the past with those addicts that came to me, they were helping me die with no apparent misgivings because at the end of the day if I did die there would always be another to take my place.

The lengths to which I would go to obtain drugs became ever more desperate. I started to go to places from where I knew few came out alive. One instance of this is clearly demonstrated when out of desperation I met with several gang members I knew to be extremely dangerous and unconcerned with who they hurt to get what they wanted.

We met in a dark alley. I was trying to score and they could see my desperation. Here was an easy mark. Most of them knew me, but do not kid yourself. A mark was a mark, money was money and loyalty was nothing more than an inconvenient thought process.

As I tried to negotiate the deal I noticed I was slowly being encircled by several members of the gang. I knew I was about to get rushed and only luck or a miracle would see me out of this. I hung on, however, continuing to try and come to a deal, so strong was the need for the drugs I sought.

As the group drew closer and cut off any possible means for escape, I realized I had to act or the next time someone heard from me would be in the obituaries. This gang had a reputation of not leaving their victims alive to potentially testify against them.

Luckily for me I had either been a witness to this type of situation or had even taken part in it before. Turning to the closest gang member I put my hand behind my back and under my coat trying to make it look like I had a gun.

I screamed "One step closer and I'll blow your f'ing head off". His one moment of hesitation was all I needed. I ran past him and sprinted towards the end of the alley. I have had dreams in which I was trying to run from something and for some reasons my legs didn't work or felt as if they were made of concrete. This is what I experienced as I ran towards the lighted street as if by reaching it I would be safe.

The light represented life. The alley behind me was death; and so with all the energy my now emaciated body could muster I sprinted for that light.

Here I received the miracle I needed, especially considering this took place around two in the morning. The traffic on the street was heavy and as I reached it I knew there would be too many possible witnesses for the gang to carry out their plans for me.

I continued to run and soon was in my vehicle. I had made it out alive. I forced a laugh and tried to convince myself that I was invincible.

Here the insanity of the disease became evident. After this close call and being so close to death that I could smell the grave, I cruised around a bit in an effort to calm down. I smoked more drugs and went to another area to search for more.

By this point my friends and family were a second thought at best. Those I had originally hung out with as fellow dealers fell by the wayside. Many were arrested, some were killed but the vast majority soon stopped returning my calls or requests to hang out. They knew I was on the way down and would have nothing to do with me because they were worried I would give them up if caught.

When considering the mind set of these supposed friends I am lucky to be alive. I have heard of way too many instances where a decision to fix a potential problem before it became serious came to fruition and someone wound up dead.

I had lost over 40 pounds and looked like a victim of cancer. My eyes were sunken into my head and my face became taut. No longer did my clothes fit and my lungs hurt from the constant intake of crack through the pipe. I was losing my family, my wellbeing and my soul.

Yet none of this mattered, nothing came before my drugs. I would be awake for days, completely strung out on cocaine. I would be at the point of having trouble controlling my body. I'd twitch and would experience paranoia and even delusions. However I was convinced that the trouble and pain I was going through would be far less than what I would have to endure if I tried to quit.

The only time I could sleep was if I passed out or collapsed. My body would force sleep in an effort to stay alive. Yet when I awoke, my first and only thought was for the drugs. I wouldn't even get out of bed. I would find the pipe wherever I had left it, usually beside me where I had dropped it when I passed out; grab a piece and fire it up. It would take several hits before I felt "right" again and then my day could start.

My days were filled only with satisfying the need for the next high. My true moments of desperation and overwhelming panic came when I would awake to find I was out of drugs. Regardless of the hour I would phone anyone I knew who might have some. If I was out of money, I would resort to begging for a hit. I would offer any possession I had that I thought may be have value, in the hopes the dealer would exchange it for drugs.

Endlessly I would ask for a front, knowing full well I didn't know when I would be able repay the loan but as with everything else the potential consequences of such actions took a back seat to satisfying that incessant need.

It was not long before this that, through ignorance; I had openly mocked and teased those that came to me in the same state I now found myself in. How pathetic I thought they were. How incredibly susceptible to any way people could exploit them. I would look down my nose at them and then sell them the thing that had put them in that state.

Now it was me, the shaking, sweaty junkie begging for a fix. I had become what had originally repulsed me. I had become a junkie. The feelings of power I used to get; the sickly boost to my ego had been replaced by the desperate need to fulfill my addiction.

I was aware of my condition and told myself I didn't care. If the feelings of shame became too much I would simply hit the pipe again and put the voices to rest.

At this point I still felt I needed to be around others while I used; as if by being with them it validated my own practices. I didn't feel so guilty because here was someone else doing the exact same thing.

It was not uncommon for me to hang around people, supplying their drugs for them, even knowing I was being used, just because I didn't want to be alone.

I was now a shell of a human being. My physical state continued to deteriorate and my soul was dying. I had stuffed and suppressed my emotions to such an extent that the thought of feeling became foreign and repulsive.

I would have been blind to not see the damage I was doing to myself. To realize the damage I was causing. The pain I was inflicting on those around me and the pain I was visiting on myself. The simple fact is that I didn't care.

I had long ago decided that the life of an addict was preferable to someone who had to live up to responsibilities, face emotions and carry themselves in a socially acceptable way.

I had resigned myself to dying and anything that brought me closer was, in my mind, the only path I saw.

It was on a sunny day. I was hanging around with one of those who used me to get free drugs. I had developed an affinity for crack and so was upset when all I could find was cocaine in powder form. Knowing that this supposed friend often used cocaine through IV I asked "What is it like when you inject?" His response was "You'll probably like it too much".

There wasn't even a moment's hesitation when I suggested we go back to his place and he introduce me to his master the needle.

Off we went. Before me lay hell and I went forth gladly; almost eagerly awaiting the inevitable end. Before this I had sworn I would never touch the needle yet when told I would like it, I charged forth.

Being a slave to the needle brought forth yet another level of hell.

Chapter 14

"The Intervention"

During the time I was trying to function at work and slowly losing that battle. I continued to complain to my doctor about ever increasing migraines, some real, some not.

After endless shots of Demerol the doctor finally suggested that I visit a pain management clinic run though the local hospital. My initial reaction was that of fear, perhaps they would uncover the truth about my migraines and that they were not as frequent as I reported.

However I went to the appointment and much to my relief and potential demise the doctors quickly gave me an almost endless amount of morphine. Once again I had taken a step up in the medications I was using. Although I had used morphine before, it was always for a very short duration. So when the opportunity came to base my addiction on this new drug of choice I jumped at the opportunity.

I wound up being part of a study that investigated the success of the clinic. I was required to maintain headache sheets that were to be updated daily and given to the medical staff when I returned bi-weekly. I, of course, filled them out moments before each appointment.

On the sheets I made it appear that the current dosage of morphine was insufficient and was always "rewarded" with an increase. To be honest, I do not know how many pills I was taking a day. It was not uncommon that I would run out of this huge amount well before my next appointment.

Having gone through withdrawal from several drugs, I can tell you that as far as I am concerned morphine and presumably heroin are the worst. When I was out of drugs I would report to Susan, who was already concerned with the amount I was taking, that I had decided to quit cold turkey.

To this day I am unsure if she believed me or knew that I had simply run out again and decided it wasn't worth the fight to point out my obvious lie.

When the times came to quit I was almost immediately cast into hell. I can still recall muscles so cramped and so painful that simply walking was at times impossible. I would lie awake for hours sweating away the pounds, my mind racing from one half hallucinations to the next as I endured more over all physical pain than at any other point in my life.

I lived in the tub for days, constantly increasing the temperature of the water to try and help with the muscle spasms. It got so bad that often I couldn't wear clothes because they simply hurt too much. Also all of my nerves seemed to stand on end and so the clothing only served to irritate this discomfort.

My mood was awful to say the least. The very slightest thing could set me off into an almost uncontrollable rage. Luckily for me and those around me, I was too weak to do anything other than hurl halfhearted insults at them

Sleep was impossible. Regardless of how exhausted I was or how worn out my body was, I simply could not sleep for any length of time. Even when I did finally slip into an uncomfortable, nightmare filled sleep, my body continued to sweat and twitch.

I honestly do not know if one can die from morphine withdrawal but at moments like those I thought I was.

All of these physical difficulties were compounded by the emotional side of things. The constant cravings almost turned me insane. I became so focused on getting more drugs that I would contact the pharmacy where I usually filled my prescriptions.

Being the good addict that I was, I would often be able to convince the pharmacist that I had simply lost my pills and he would give me a smaller portion to carry me through until my next appointment.

Mustering all of my remaining strength I would almost crawl to the car and make my way to the pharmacy. Sweaty and looking gaunt I would bounce from foot to foot as I waited impatiently to get my pills.

Grabbing a drink on the way out of the store I would quickly start stuffing pills down my throat the second I got inside the vehicle. Imagine the desperation as I watched the clock, waiting for the medication to take effect.

When it finally did, everything was once again right in the world. The lessons I should have learned having gone through this ordeal, quickly were displaced by the comfort I received from having satisfied my addiction.

While attending the pain management clinic I constantly complained about sleepless nights. In truth I think I requested a pill for that to help in those times when I ran out of morphine. So armed with the latest device for self-destruction, I set out to slowly kill myself. I would mix morphine and sleeping pills to the point where remembering how many I had taken over the course of the day was impossible.

One time Susan and I traveled to Hawaii. Although I have no recollection, she tells me that once while driving I nodded off and drove towards an oncoming semi and had she not grabbed the wheel we would be dead.

Did this stop me from continuing on the path I had chosen? Of course not!

When the idea of using the needle came to me as a real possibility I gave up on life. I had always carried in the back of my mind the idea that at some time I would quit using. That, as I had done in the past, I would be able to get out of trouble and this philosophy carried into my drug use.

Mike and I returned to his house where he kept a few rigs around and my crash course in skin breaking began. I can recall being nervous.

It was as if some part of me was trying to scream out in horror at what I was about to do.

Yet here before me was a chance to increase my buzz. I had been told this would lead to another level of high, so without a second thought I took off my jacket, watched the mixing process and eagerly waited.

Mike had to fix first of course. He used the excuse he had to make sure his hands were steady, yet I knew he was just ensuring he got the first taste.

I looked away as the needle entered my arm, and then a sensation of bliss washed over me. I will avoid describing the sensation in too much detail for fear of triggering that obsession. It is worthy of noting that even nine months since my last use, just the thought of that first experience releases adrenalin and temptation.

After a while I decided I had to return home. Truth be told I do not know how long I had been away but felt an overwhelming need to go back. Armed with a few loaded rigs that Mike had prepared for me I went home.

I have no recollection of the drive home; I think it was during the day, however even now I cannot be sure. What resonates in my mind is the fact that I was driving in this condition and never once gave a second thought to the fact I could kill myself or someone else.

Once again I was presented with the fact that God was watching out for me and it is only now as I relate this to you that it becomes apparent.

Returning home I hesitated in showing my wife the loaded syringes fearing her reaction. She had often said that she would never touch needles, just as I had. Yet when I did finally show her she seemed eager to try and so we spent the evening injecting.

I was not very adept at the process but for some reason she was. As I had done with Mike, I would look away as Susan found the vein and pumped the poison into my body. This officially ended my recent attempt at drug dealing.

The needle quickly became my lover and my soul mate. If I was in a pinch I would defer to the pipe but always longed for the needle.

Soon my days were filled with the search for powder, the acquisition of needles and the using of the drug.

It was not long before some of the terrible side effects came along as well. At first I would experience stomach cramps and vomiting if I injected too much. There were several times where after an injection my body would start to twitch uncontrollably. One time as I sat there kidding myself I was enjoying the latest hit, the walls looked like they were covered with different colors that ran down like wet paint.

Oblivious or at least uncaring about the damage I was doing to my body I would express how funny this latest reaction was. Isn't it funny what is happening to me I thought. Oblivious to the damage I was doing to my brain, I would lie there in a stupor feeling good about the choice to switch to the needle.

Along with the need and the desire to satisfy my new master came the chaos that followed. Quickly I slipped into ever increasing acts of depravity. Soon all of my credit cards were maxed out. My wife and I had borrowed money from her parents several times under the guise that we needed it to pay bills when in fact the only place the majority of the money went to was whatever dealer we were using at the time.

Countless times I would meet my potential end in a dark alley, focused only on the product I was in search for. Regardless of the fact that I had seen many deals go bad in places just like the alleys I frequented and having almost been killed by a gang in just such a place, I didn't hesitate when an alley or dark area was the suggested meeting place.

Hours were wasted by the phone waiting for someone to call or to go "Shopping", a term used by drug dealers when they need to reload. Days filled slowly killing myself and watching my wife do it as well, slipped by without any real recognition. My weight dropped to about 125 pounds, I weight 225 now. Once again my clothes stopped fitting and yet with all this evidence of my impending demise at hand, I carried forward.

It was so easy to score, I was so well versed in the street lingo required to pick up. Within drug circles and among dealers and their customers there is a language that has developed. It helps the dealers and the customers potentially identify police when going about their business.

For instance I would call a dealer and ask him if he was interested in rock climbing for an hour. Translation I wanted an hour (one gram) of Crack (rock). There are many, many other examples of this type of thing but you had to know them. If you were unfamiliar with the lingo at best it meant you didn't get what you wanted, at worst you may be mistaken for a cop and simply killed.

So it went for almost a year. I kidded myself the whole time that I was fooling everyone. Regardless of the times when I convinced my family to take our son so my wife and I could work things out and regardless of the obvious physical and emotional deterioration I was utterly convinced that no one knew that my wife and I spent the vast majority of our time in the basement of our house, growing ever more paranoid and yet continuing to use.

During all of this, my contact with my family became less and less. This also included my friend Bruce who had recently moved from Vancouver to Edmonton, a city about three hours from where I was living. I didn't know it at the time but this move would ultimately play a major role in the recovery I am now experiencing.

After a year or so Susan and I received a visit from her mother. It does me no good to rant about her parents but I must admit that they are a different breed of people. They have money and seem to think that those that do not are below them. I do not come from a wealthy family so obviously I was not liked from the moment they learned that.

I had never been one to keep my mouth shut when something irritated me so I had quickly developed a relationship with my wife's mother that was cold at best.

Although the majority of my dealing was behind me, I still had a few unpaid debts to collect on. As well, my wife had become uneasy about the amount we were doing and so together we decided to keep a written journal of not only our usage but also those who owed us money.

This alone should make it abundantly clear how messed up we were. In the past the last thing I would do would be to commit to paper anything that could be used against me, especially anything like obvious drug dealing that could land me in jail.

Yet I carried forth truly believing that having this written evidence was in my best interest and a great idea.

At some point during her visit my mother in law, suspicious of our drug use, found the book while searching the house. Little did I know at the time but she planned an intervention.

A few days later she disappeared from the house and I knew something was up. Susan and I talked about where her mother had gone and somehow through the haze of drug use came to the conclusion that she had gone to my parents to bring them back so that they could confront us about our using.

Desperation ran through my mind. I had to escape. I could not, would not, allow someone to get in the way of my using. However much to my chagrin my mother in law had taken the car keys before leaving.

I turned to the only solution I knew. I grabbed a handful of morphine, the exact number of which I have no clue and several sleeping pills.

Moments later, when the effects of the medication hadn't kicked in, I topped up the first dosage with more of the same.

Finally the relaxing feeling I sought came over me and I proceeded to wait calmly for the perceived attack. I recall thinking that if they're going to take me down I was going down with a serious buzz.

One by one the opposing forces entered the house. I got set for battle and sized up the combatants. In addition to my parents and my wife's mother was my eldest brother and his wife. The evening even included a surprise guest in the appearance of my wife's father who having been informed of the intervention days before and had driven in from Revelstoke B.C.

By now everyone and everything was moving in slow motion. I was so incredibly high that as those that had gathered spoke to us, their voices were almost unintelligible.

Without hesitation the questioning began. To the best of my recollection it went like this:

"Are you guys on drugs?" Our obvious response was "Who, us?" I think it was at that point my sister in law asked to see our arms. Somehow she had figured out pretty quickly I was a slave to the needle.

Although I had continued to use the syringe my wife had reverted to the pipe, especially when her mother was around as she would often inspect Susan's arms long before the intervention.

Wanting this to end as quickly as possible so I could get my car keys back and go score, I showed everyone the one arm I didn't use. Not being fooled, my sister in law quickly asked to see the other and also my legs.

At that point I knew I was busted but for some reason I was starting to care less and less. In fact the whole situation was somehow becoming comical. People's faces started to contort, often their voices would range from a very high pitched squeal to a low almost foghorn quality. I didn't associate this with drugs, being so mixed up and simply tried to fight the urge to giggle.

When I finally revealed my arms and my legs the mess I found even managed to cut through the fog in my mind and made me wince. Open sores, infected injection sites and old track marks were evident.

I tried to cover the obvious wounds by saying that I had recently injured myself with the lawn mower. In my mind this was a completely plausible excuse. Regardless of the fact the marks were made from needles, in my confused state I truly believed that the sores I saw were in fact from the source I blamed them on. When they all scoffed at my obvious lie I was offended.

In fact, I realized, I was offended by this whole evening thus far. Who were these people who stated they cared for me and then had the audacity to question my word? At the core of the matter, who were they to try and stop me from using. Didn't they know who I was? Didn't they know what difficulties I had faced in my life and as such deserved to indulge every once in a while.

If I wanted to abandon my life, my son, my business and my soul what business was it of theirs? How dare they come into my house and try and save my life?

I started to see red. I was close to attacking whoever was closest. After all wasn't I the true victim here? Do not speak to me of the pain I am causing. I was not sure how but this must be their fault, so by what right do they now try and intercede?

Had it not been for the heavy dosage of drugs in my system I surely would have gotten violent.

As it was, the last few things I remember from that evening was trying to convince them that my wife and I had tried drugs a few times and had given them up. We were asked when we had stopped. I turned to Susan and said "Wasn't it around June?"

At that point the full effect of the drugs kicked in. I nodded off and stopped breathing.

Chapter 15

"Insanity Takes Hold"

A blinding white light, incoherent voices and a feeling of lethargy welcomed me as I climbed back to the land of the living. I was greeted by a scene of confusion. Apparently I was in a hospital bed.

Except for my father I recognized no one around me as I groggily took in my surroundings.

For the time being I had absolutely no recollection of how I had gotten to the hospital. In fact, I don't think I could have told you my own name. I saw my father staring at me, a mix of relief, sadness and anger flashed across his face.

Doctors and nurses buzzed around me like industrious bees and for a while I felt as if I was a bystander watching them work on some poor sucker that had gotten himself into trouble. It took several minutes before I realized that sucker was me.

It strikes me as a sort of sad and yet funny thing that even as the realization of what had happened dawned on me I wasn't scared or even really upset. It was if I had surrendered to the concept of my inevitable death. I had come close but would know what to do next time to ensure my demise.

The doctor noticed me coming around and greeted me with a gruff "Decided to hang around for a while did you?" Instantly I was filled with contempt, I was still trying to adjust to what had happened and yet here this doctor was demonstrating such an unbelievable insensitivity.

"You know, for quite a while there we didn't think you were going to make it" he continued to admonish. "Someone must have been watching out for you".

I wish now that I could have replied with the knowledge I have recently learned that yes in fact someone was and had always been watching out for me. In fact this was just another event in a long string of incidents that proved God had my back through all of my life.

I was attached to tubes, hooked to monitors and was apparently receiving the royal treatment. The questioning intensified. "What did you take?" the doctor asked. I responded "Nothing." So completely unaware of how dire my circumstances were I still thought I could bluff my way through this predicament.

After all, this was simply another hurdle I had to clear before I could return to my life of debauchery. I decided I would humor the medical staff so long as I could get out of the hospital in a reasonable time and get back to the needle.

It was not long before the medical staff became aware of the fact I had a child at home. It is only in recollection that I remember the disapproving look that crossed the nurse's face as this was revealed. I didn't know it at the time but this revelation made her responsible for contacting social services.

I do not know how long I remained in the emergency room. For me time was a concept I really couldn't grasp. After a while of treatment I was finally admitted and moved to one of the wards.

Later I would find out the particulars of what had happened at home that led up to me being brought to the hospital.

The questioning of Susan's and my drug use was directed at her long enough that it took some time for someone to notice my condition. Upon realizing I was in a bad way my eldest brother and my father transported me to the hospital in my father's vehicle. I had in fact stopped breathing; in fact my heart may have stopped.

Although I do not remember it, apparently I had returned to consciousness shortly after arriving at the hospital and became violent.

That is, as violent as one in my condition could be. The nurse simply swatted away my feeble attempts to hit her and fight the treatment I was receiving. She had seen many before me in this state and sadly enough I am sure has seen many more since.

Impervious to my verbal assault she took me into emergency and it is only through the measures of the doctors and nurses as well as God that I am here today. Later I would learn that I was perhaps one pill or simply a few minutes away from death.

The infections from the injection sites, mostly those on my legs, had gotten so bad that the concern was the infection may have permanently damaged my heart. Although later tests would reveal that my heart had somehow managed to not be injured, I still wonder about its real condition.

The first day was the worst. Until a full medical work up could be completed I was deprived of any medication. That of course included the morphine. Withdrawal from morphine starts very quickly after ceasing the drug. In addition to the fact that I felt like I was back in jail I was going through awful tremors, sweats and hallucinations.

The staff at the hospital had no intention of coddling me and was in fact very short when speaking or dealing with me. Perhaps they understood the precious gift of life and were upset at someone trying so hard to throw that gift away or maybe they had seen so many like I that they were in fact desensitized to the whole process.

Either way, attempts on my part to manipulate the nursing staff to approach the doctors on my behalf to acquire something, anything to ease my pains fell on deaf ears.

After a few days of hell I finally saw an addictions specialist, who decided to start me on a taper down off the morphine. I was ecstatic. I paid no heed to the fact that eventually I was expected to stop the morphine all together and was only interested in the fact that I was being given what I wanted, more drugs.

By this point I was so weak from the infection and the withdrawal that I needed assistance to use the washroom. I had reduced myself to being dependent on someone to walk me three feet across a room. However within a half hour of receiving my first full dosage of morphine I was ready to resume my life.

I was impressed by my apparent ability to snap back from this encounter with death and immediately perceived I must, in fact, be indestructible.

This is where the insanity of addiction once again becomes apparent. In relaying my next action to you I shudder at the true depravity of the disease.

As soon as I could walk again I made my way to the closest pay phone, contacted a dealer I knew and tried to convince him to bring me some coke, some crack, anything to the hospital.

Being the true "friend" he was the only thing that in fact stopped him from complying with my outlandish request was that I had no money on me and I was looking for a front.

It is obvious to me now that Susan's parents did not approve of me. As I have said before, money is everything to them. By me not having much of it I was apparently less and therefore not worthy of their daughter and even worse yet, certainly not worth being a member of their family.

I fully accept my responsibility for my actions and do not blame them for the fact that their reaction to this newest situation was less than supportive. After all who am I to judge how one should react to this type of thing. As I will relate later, their actions took on a whole new level of underhandedness.

Days crawled by and my family was supportive. I cannot recall if Susan came to visit me in the hospital even once. My mother later told me she did in fact visit several times. Although I didn't know it at the time Susan and her parents were hard at work destroying any evidence of her involvement, proceeding towards a divorce and in fact making plans to take Susan and my son out of province.

Later I would learn that it was during my time in the hospital that Susan's parents tried to take her back to Salmon Arm BC and have her enter treatment. When Susan declined she was told that unless she did what she was told her parents would disown her.

Susan continued to refuse so her parents made good on their threat, packed their belongings and went home.

It still bothers me to this day that they not only abandoned their daughter but they were just as quick to leave my son behind. They knew full well the depths that Susan and I had sunk to, yet they were willing to leave a one year old child in Susan's care.

In fact the only effort they made to ensure our son's safety was to make a couple of futile efforts to dump him on Susan's sister.

The wagons had been circled and it would be quite some time before I realized I was not part of that circle.

One day my eldest brother and his wife showed up at the hospital for a visit. I had recently received my daily dosage of morphine and so was on top of the world, ready to joke about and laugh off the situation at hand.

Unbeknownst to me they had also brought their pastor with them to try and talk some sense into me. The pastor, who would later play a significant role in my return to God, had in fact had his own difficulties with alcohol earlier in life.

As such, he understood that unless I was ready to get help his visit would be unproductive. However my family was reaching out not knowing what else to do and so probably as much for them as for me he accompanied them that day to the hospital.

After a few minutes of talking with my brother and his wife the pastor came in. I recognized him and all at once felt betrayed. Of all the audacity! To spring this on me now. Couldn't they see the turmoil I was in? Didn't they understand my difficulties? Didn't they know that at that point I simply could not have cared one iota for their emotional wellbeing?

I instantly went into defensive position as the pastor approached. As kindly as he could he ask me how I was feeling, I replied, in a short tone "fine."

With understanding, he asked me if I wished to tell him why I had wound up where I was. I couldn't believe the insensitivity of this man. Was he mocking me? Obviously he knew why I was there or else he wouldn't have known to come to the hospital.

I replied "Let's not play games! Obviously you know why I am here."

I can still recall his kind smile as he patted me on the shoulder wished me luck and offered to be there if I ever felt I wanted his help. He then bid my brother and his wife a good day and left.

Through this I can once again see that constantly my footsteps were dogged by God and he had attempted, once again, to lend a helping hand. However I would not be ready for some time after this to accept that help.

I spent the next few days making the most of my surroundings. Slowly I was able to get the nursing staff to ease up on me somewhat and a few, I think, I even manipulated into feeling sorry for me. This combined with the fact that although I was craving cocaine I was having morphine hand delivered to me daily made the situation bearable.

I had television to occupy my time and free drugs, what could be better I thought.

So, growing happy, I once again subconsciously found a way to sabotage it. The morphine was now being reduced and I simply couldn't have that. I mean did the staff at the hospital not understand how important my buzz was? Who were they to try and get me healthy anyways?

So, feeling deprived, I spoke to my hospital roommate who also had a lengthy career of drug abuse. I was than schooled in how to crush the morphine tablets they were giving me and how to prepare them for injection.

One day, after getting my morning dosage, I set forth to execute this plan. Sticking my hands several times and exposing myself to heaven knows what infections, medications or diseases I found a way to bypass the cover on the used syringe receptacle and finally was "rewarded" with a needle.

It is only now that I realize that this is more than likely the way I contracted Hepatitis C. This disease would later play a very significant role in my life.

Grabbing the spoon I had used from the night before I went into the bathroom and attempted to get ready for the injection.

I must have been in there for some time and was noticed missing because it was not long before the door to the washroom swung open revealing a nurse with a rather angry look on her face. She knew what I was up to and probably could not believe the depths of my insanity.

Here I was fresh from an overdose, having been on the verge of death, infection and open sores on my legs and I was trying to inject myself with a used syringe.

Being the good addict that I was I immediately mixed an attitude of disdain for her accusations with lies. Before the questioning had started I had managed to hide the needle, however I still had the spoon. No I was not trying to inject myself. I was simply being a good patient and had planned to wash the spoon simply on the basis I didn't want the staff at the hospital to have to worry about it.

In fact, I thought, I should be commended on my thoughtfulness.

I continued to try and defend myself even after it became apparent that the nurse did not believe me. I even went so far as to challenge her to do a drug test that would obviously prove my innocence. Since I had yet to inject I thought I had her and there was nothing she could do about it.

As it turned out, she decided, with the advice of a doctor, to do the drug test after all. Apparently she saw through my bluff. Regardless of the fact that since I had been injecting cocaine before entering the hospital and that the staff was giving me daily dosages of morphine they used this supposed test results to prove my guilt. In short order I was asked to leave the hospital. I was offered an opportunity to see an addictions specialist through the hospital but quickly turned it down. After all only addicts need to see an addictions specialist and I thought I was anything but an addict.

Even in the face of having given up this opportunity to get clean and avail myself of the help being offered I still was able to convince myself that I was the one who had been wronged.

By this point in my addiction the insanity had taken such a hold that I could view instances such as this and truly believe I was the victim. I could see some of the damage I was causing both in my life and in the lives of those around me and yet was able to perceive myself as having to deal with all of these heartaches on my own.

I had convinced myself that my using was not only acceptable but that anyone having to endure what I had been through would turn to drugs as well; as such how could anyone hold me accountable for my actions?

I was quickly running out of options. The system I had taken advantage of for so many years was crumbling under my feet. I was heading towards bottom at an ever increasing pace and was completely oblivious to it all.

The strength of my denial was extreme and, as I would later find out, only served to hamper any efforts to get clean.

I was now en route to living on the street, giving up my family and all of the possessions I had coveted so jealously, and yet I continued.

The next few months in my life would prove to be the most trying times I had ever faced.

Chapter 16

"Chaos Ensues"

By the time I had been asked to leave the hospital I was sickly, under weight and emotionally drained. It was my plan to get as high as possible as fast as possible. Susan picked me up and I went home to get some clothing.

By this time social services were investigating the case. Since someone had overdosed in a house with a child they had to look into it. While they were doing their investigating I was not allowed to reside at the house. My son and my time with him were second to the need to feed my addiction.

To be exact I wound up giving up my wife, my son, my career and all of my worldly possessions because at the time they were not as important as the drugs I sought and the lifestyle I pursued.

Since those days I have heard many say "I lost my family" or "I lost my career". For me I didn't lose a single thing while lost in my addiction. I gave it all up. I forfeited it all because it got in the way of my using.

Relationships and responsibilities were simply a hindrance to my consumption of drugs. Perhaps that demonstrates the hold addiction can have on you when the crucial things in your life pale in comparison to the all-consuming need to get high.

I returned home briefly. My son was being looked after by my brother and sister in law which was fine by me because I didn't have to worry about him. I gathered some clothing together and headed over to my parents. On the way I was able to manipulate Susan into stopping by the pharmacy. The pharmacist, totally unaware of what had transpired, filled all my prescriptions. I walked out of the store with a fresh bottle of Tylenol #3, Morphine and sleeping pills.

I was well stocked and since I had already taken some pills in the pharmacy I felt I would soon once again be invulnerable.

At the time I was unaware of the influence Susan's parents had over her and that she had been instructed to keep her distance from me. I was surprised when she repeatedly told me that we would stick together; that the both of us would get through this and that nothing was going to break up our family.

Little did I know that her family had convinced her to follow a different plan altogether. In fact by this point plans were being made to pursue a divorce and somehow figure out how to get my name off the title to the house.

Upon arriving at my parents, guidelines were handed down as to what behavior was expected from me. There was to be no drug use, in or out of the house, and certainly no drug paraphernalia on the premises.

I quickly agreed to these conditions, simply wanting to ensure a roof over my head. My parents asked that I sign a contract that outlined these rules. I would have signed it in blood had they wanted me to. All I was concerned with was getting downstairs to top up my buzz. Even as I put pen to paper I knew I had no intention of honoring this contract.

I found my way to the basement of the house and quickly downed some more pills! I can't honestly say which ones simply because it did not matter. Here I was fresh out of the hospital having been treated for an overdose that nearly killed me and my prime concern was increasing and maintaining my high.

I nodded off for a while and was awakened by my parents coming down the stairs. Apparently Susan had left and they were coming down to talk to me. I lit up a cigarette and tried in vain to speak to them. I was slurring my words and in fact kept falling asleep, oblivious to the danger that the smoke in my hand posed.

When questioned about my inability to stay awake I told my parents it was a residual effect from the treatment at the hospital. I remember being quizzed on why I had to leave the hospital and made it seem like I was the victim of some plot.

Obviously the staff was out to get rid of me as they had unjustly kicked me out.

After a short amount of time my parents gave up trying to talk to someone who was almost comatose and returned upstairs. I do not recall how long I slept; however I did awake at one point to find that Susan had returned. Finding me in this condition in the basement, pills scattered all over the table in front of me, she had gathered them all up and was trying to leave.

I couldn't have that! This was my supply she was messing with. Most of the following events have been relayed to me by those that witnessed the chaos because I simply cannot remember.

Apparently I chased her up the stairs screaming at her to return the medication, trying to impress upon her the absolute need I had for the pills and the possible damage she could do to me if she took them.

Shortly verbal assault turned physical as it became clear that she had no intention of returning the drugs I sought.

As she rained blows upon me I tried to restrain her as she tried to make her way out to her vehicle. Finally I wore her down and she threw the pill bottles at me. By this time the whole family was aware of the scuffle. Since my brother and sister in law lived next door with their three kids everyone was witness to the depravity.

Returning to the house, pills in hand, I attempted to gain entry. Having feared for themselves my family had locked the door. In my confused state I didn't give a second thought to trying to kick the door in. Once again I was indignant that people could not see the plight I was in and were being so insensitive.

Susan had followed me back up onto the front porch launching her own verbal assault. From next door my sister in law came out and confronted Susan on her drug abuse. Unbeknownst to me Susan and her parents were already denying any real involvement with drugs and that any drug use that had gone on prior to my hospitalization was done primarily by me.

There they stood in a screaming match, my sister in law attempting to make Susan face the fact she also had a problem and Susan denying it for all she was worth. After a brief verbal exchange Susan threw a punch at my sister in law which was quickly pushed aside.

Grabbing Susan's arm my sister in law turned her arm over exposing several track marks asking: "If you are not doing drugs then what are these?" Susan than retreated to the vehicle screaming she would have my sister in law charged with assault. Much like I did, Susan saw herself as a victim who held close ties to denial.

Before all of this had happened Bruce had been contacted in Edmonton and without a second's hesitation grabbed some belongings, jumped into his car and made the three hour drive to Calgary. This is the type of guy Bruce is. A friend in need! There are no second thoughts. As a friend you help and so that is what he planned to do.

Having spoken to him after all of this, he still comments on how he was totally unprepared for what lay in wait for him. How could anyone new to a situation like this be ready?

Arriving in Calgary he was shocked to find his friend and his friend's wife completely emaciated, strung out and in the case of his friend actively using and making no apology for his behavior.

Try as he might to make me get help I was totally resistant to his pleas. He then worked closely with my family to try and show me where I was headed and the damage I was doing to my family and myself. Although I knew what he said made sense at the time I couldn't care less.

This is when Susan's parents went into overdrive with their plans. They had returned from BC to "fix things". One way or another they were going to collect their child, minimize the financial damage that may be done and return home.

It was quite some time later I learned about the true depths they were willing to go to so that they, as well as Susan, could perpetuate the denial. They started conjuring up a story that Susan had only tried drugs once and in fact before having met me had never tried hard drugs in her life. A statement I know, through conversations with Susan prior to all of this happening, to be false.

As mentioned before the primary concern was for the financial aspect of things. Before I met Susan she had purchased her own home. Obviously when I moved in, well before our marriage, I started paying a portion of the mortgage. Shortly after taking up residence with Susan she transferred half ownership of the house to me and this drove her parents nuts. Especially now that they wanted to get rid of me they were most concerned with the fact that if they sold the house I would be entitled to half the proceeds.

As such plan "A" came into effect. One day Susan's mother approached Bruce and asked him to convince me to sign over my half of the house. If he did so she would "make it worth his while."

Attempting to hide his horror at her actions my friend inquired "How much would that get me?" and was quickly offered $10,000.00. An offer adamantly declined. Once again Bruce had stuck up for his friend. Even while I was out attempting to kill myself he was trying to watch out for my best interests.

When plan "A" didn't work Susan's parents resorted to plan "B". Plan "B" involved getting me to sign not only the house over but all of the possessions inside the house. Most of those possessions had been purchased on my credit cards. Yet when they offered me $5000.00 cash to sign it all away I jumped at the chance.

The agreement of the $5000.00 was quickly put into writing and I couldn't wait to sign it. Susan promised another $10,000.00 after the sale of the house. Since this was a few years ago now, I suppose I should stop holding my breath in anticipation of that check.

They knew an active addict couldn't resist that amount of money and took full advantage of my situation. Obviously there is no doubt about the part I played in all of this but to this day the type of mentality that allows you to not only take advantage of someone's illness but also feel justified while doing it sickens me.

Needless to say the $5000.00 paid for three days in a hotel and the remainder went into my lungs and up my arm. When I left the hotel three days later I had approximately $100.00 left. The only reason I had that much left was due to the fact I had to give cash deposit when I checked in.

The chaos intensified from there. Occasionally I would guilt my parents into allowing me to return home after the latest time I had been caught using drugs and would once again have a roof over my head. This, of course, would not last long. To this day I do not know how many times I tried to live there, continuing to use and attempting to fool my parents.

Social services were nearing the end of their investigation and it didn't look good for me. Somehow Susan had by now been able to stop using. Social services demanded that we both complete a parenting group and contact their offices daily for random drug testing.

Susan completed all the requirements and I did none. Once again it was simply too much effort to try and comply when I had such a hectic schedule of debauchery to maintain.

I recall several times, moments after "hitting" calling to see if there was a drug test that day. On the occasions that I was told there would be I simply told them I would fail anyway and in that I once again not only failed myself but also my son.

By this time I had lost all interest in anything outside of using. I would do or say anything to ensure I could remain high. When the time came for Susan and me to go to family court to decide what should be done with our son I was late for the court date.

I had spent the previous night at my parents' house, smoking and injecting myself into oblivion. When Susan called to see where I was my mother awoke me from my stupor. I hit the pipe several times to get myself right and called a cab. By the time I reached the court I was already "jonesing" for another hit since the ride took over half an hour.

I didn't even bother reporting to the appropriate court before finding the washroom and topping up. Finally I felt well enough to go to court. I saw Susan sitting there, obvious relief that I had shown up written all over her face.

Sweating away and twitching I tried to sit still while I waited for them to call our name. Since it seemed to take forever I went back to the washroom several times to maintain my high. Here I was in court, about to supposedly fight for my son and was still more interested in getting high.

Finally our names were called and Susan stood before the court, opened her mouth and let loose a string of lies. Lies that included the "fact" she only used a couple of times and how it was my fault she used in the first place.

Since Susan had completed the requirements of social services and I had not she was awarded full custody of our son. The amount of times she assured me she would not take my son from me after that is countless. In fact she was still promising me this right up to the point that she sold the house and moved with our son to BC.

Susan had full custody. I was lost in my addiction and there was nothing either I or my family could do about it. Excluding one or two brief visits, my parents haven't seen their grandson since his move to BC.

I dove head first into using at this point and that is when the seizures increased. As I have said I was set to kill myself. I remember several times about to inject wondering if the amount I was about to take would kill me. My next thought? "Huh, who cares?" I remember being upset when it didn't and immediately fixed again.

The seizures had become so regular that I probably was having one in every three shots. From what I have been told it was extremely ugly to witness. I would drop to the ground thrashing around as if I was having an epileptic attack. After several minutes of this I would slow down, seem to come too but unfortunately for those around me this is when things went from bad to worse.

After each seizure I would come out of it and directly into a psychotic episode. I still do not remember anything but brief memories of being attacked and so believing I had to defend myself I would attack anyone near me.

There would be times I would awake to find police holding me down.

One of the worst instances of this was the time I seized in front of my son and my mother. My mother tried to hold me as I thrashed about. My son, about one year old, screaming in horror and crying, not knowing what was happening to his daddy. Coming out of the seizure I launched a physical attack on my mother, hitting her several times and finally fleeing into a nearby alley.

The police and ambulance were called. Eventually I came to and returned home to find them all waiting for me. I had no recollection of the events that led up to this point and was surprised to find an ambulance and several police cars waiting for me.

The police seated me in the living room and asked what I had been taking? Falling back on my usual concept of coming clean if already busted I admitted to using cocaine. One of the officers asked me where the remainder was. This is where instinct for survival and an overall lack of desire to return to jail kicked in and I successfully lied that I had used it all.

The emergency staff recommended several times that I accompany them to the hospital but knowing they could not make me go I continued to refuse until they finally gave up.

It would be some time before I realized the physical and emotional damage I had done to my loved ones on that day.

Even now as I relate this to you I weep with the shame and guilt that plagues me to this day. My family had stood by me through this all. My son was innocent, dependent upon his father to teach him about life and look out for his best interests and yet here I was abusing drugs and abusing them.

God forgive me. God please help me forgive myself.

Even with this in mind it was not the end of my using. Even after all that had happened I still was not truly aware of the depths to which I had sunk.

It was reported to me that each time I had an episode like this not only did I endanger those around me but I ran the risk of permanently damaging my brain. There may come a time when I enter into a psychotic state and never come out.

With all of this in mind I continued to use. I continued to sink deeper and I continued to seek a way off this planet; away from my responsibilities, away from expectations, away from my fears of trust, relieved of my lack of self-worth and most importantly liberated from my emotions once and for all.

I had farther to fall.

Chapter 17

"Missed Opportunities"

So this is what bottom is like. It was an endless cycle of using and depravity. Your whole day is consumed with the need to find and the need to use.

By this point I was completely lost in my addiction; thoughts of recovery were as foreign as the ability to fly. I had surrendered to the idea that I was going to die this way. An overdose, a deal gone bad, at this point it did not matter. I was not afraid of dying so much as I was far more afraid of continuing to live.

I spent the majority of my time driving through town, finding parking spots and vacant lots to shoot up or hit the pipe. I had no regard for those I endangered when I drove nor did I have any concern for my own personal wellbeing.

Addiction does not have a conscience.

Truly I struggle to demonstrate what the mind set of someone so lost in their addiction is like. Misgivings about hurting others or misgivings about delving into a certain action to attain drugs comes a far second to the need to get and use more.

During this time I was so completely wrapped up in my pursuit of the grave that I missed my son's first birthday. I stood by as my marriage deteriorated and I watched my family toil under the weight of my inevitable death.

Later my mother would relate how those around her told her she had to cut me out of her life, do not enable him. It broke my heart as she told me how she would always reply to this type of comment.

"I know he is going to die but I would rather he die in my basement than on a street corner or in an alley somewhere."

The entire time I was sinking lower I knew full well the pain I was causing, the distance I was creating in the relationships that used to be the most important. The damage to my body and the fact I could almost hear my soul crying, was not enough to make me want to quit.

My solution was to simply use more. I would turn to my master for help in quieting the voices, removing myself from the pain, guilt and shame. When those voices, those fears and that understanding of my situation became too obvious I would seek help from drugs.

The seeming endless cycle would continue. I would feel that emotion that I regarded as evil and I would turn to self-medication; regardless of the cost I would do whatever it took. Then, as I would sober up, the realization of my actions and the emotional difficulty accompanying that realization would return and so I would once again fix.

I had gone from needing to be around others while using to the point where I hated anyone being near me. This disdain for company would be prevalent whether I was using or not. I tried to tell myself that I had simply grown tired of people trying to take advantage of me for drugs.

I envisioned myself as a victim, thinking that all of those I surrounded myself with while getting high were nothing but parasites waiting to use me. Not once did I recognize the fact I was exactly the same. I too would rip someone off in a deal or try and scam a dealer if it meant free drugs.

Those that I had called friend in the circle of drug users were nothing more to me than someone to lessen my guilt with, someone to drag down with me and most importantly someone that may provide some free drugs.

There were many times, six or seven at least, where I would enter detox. The truth about this is not once did I ever enter with a true desire to get clean. Most of the time I would go into a center only to get people off my back; to try and get some reprieve from what I considered to be their constant nagging and obvious inability to understand my plight.

More often than not I would go to detox simply because I had nothing left to pawn, nothing left to trade and certainly no money. At the time my biggest fear in life was not having more drugs, it was running out. I went to detox so that I could get the limited amount of Valium they sometimes offered in the first few days of drying out. I went there because they could help with the hell of withdrawal that was approaching.

Not once did I enter detox without the idea that as soon as I got money again I would return to using.

I remember the first time going into a detox center. The feelings of insecurity I tried to hide behind false bravado. I mean after all did these people not know who I was? I was nothing like those I saw around me. It amazes me that I could so easily look down on those around me in this setting. I would openly sneer at those I saw underweight, scared and scarred. Needle marks riddling their arms, their faces gaunt and their eyes wild with a desperation I had never seen before.

In all of that time not once did it occur to me that I could stand before a mirror and see someone in the same predicament. I had only to look at my own arms to see the same scars.

I had only to look inside myself to know I shared the same feelings of desperation.

Detoxification centers are often a reflection of life on the street. Obviously there are fewer things to worry about like food and somewhere to sleep. In the center I was in, the staff did their best to eliminate people who might cause violence or steal.

However the truth of the matter is this was an entire building full of people totally lost in their addiction. The survival mode was still in full effect and those who stayed there were not above stealing your clothes and without a doubt one often had to watch their back during their stay.

While I was there we were made to go to meetings held by local twelve step programs. I remember the utter disdain I had for those that came to share. They would regale us with stories of how bad it got for them, how only after hitting bottom would they finally start to look for a way out of the mess they had found.

They would tell us things like "It was not too long ago that I was sitting where you people are now." What audacity I thought. How could they even pretend to know what I had experienced? I was so incredibly blind to the fact that these people had been exactly where I was. Perhaps they had followed a different path to the bottom but the pain and isolation, the true depravity and sense of being dead long before you stopped breathing, they had all experienced.

As soon as they began to talk I would close my mind and my heart to their pleas that we all simply try and get by one day at a time. With great sarcasm I thought I bet I could get them to all use again. I bet that if given half a chance they would be on the other end of a needle or a pipe in five seconds flat.

At the time I certainly had no intention of listening to anyone that I perceived to be judging me. After all I was only here, killing time, until my next fix.

In all the times I ever entered a detox center I only ever once stayed the recommended amount of time.

One time in particular I was outside having a smoke; talking to a guy I had met at the center, a fellow skin breaker like me named Peter. He and I had spent most of our time reminiscing about how great drugs were, how much we missed the buzz, each one of us trying to convince the other about how great we were by describing in detail those things we had done in our addiction.

As we talked endlessly about our using I happened to mention that I wished we could leave and score. Peter was new to the city and so didn't know as many people as I did in the circle of drug users and suppliers. I mentioned how if I had any cash I would leave the center immediately. After all, I could contact any of the many dealers I knew right from the detox building and have them meet me close by. I even went so far as to mention the fact I knew one dealer that would take cartons of cigarettes in exchange for drugs.

Peter's eyes lit up. It was if I had just told him he had won a million dollars. "I have a credit card" he said. I was dumbfounded! Why hadn't he mentioned this earlier?

I asked him "Why don't we just take a cash advance form your card?" "I can't get cash advances from it but we can go buy smokes" he replied.

With that we were gone. For some reason we felt the need to make up an elaborate story about how Peter was coming to stay with me at my parent's house and how they had found a rehabilitation center for the two of us; and so with concocted lie in hand we asked the staff to release us.

Of course it was an obviously poor lie and in the end didn't really matter. The staff was there to help those who wanted help not baby sit and regulate those of us who were not interested in getting clean.

In hindsight I find it odd that we would even bother to come up with an excuse for leaving. Both of us knew the rules and we each knew we could leave at any time. We were both so eager to get out and get high that I am surprised we even spent the time it took to come up with the story in the first place.

As the staff was processing Peter's release I used the payphone to reach the dealer. I can vividly remember the trepidation I felt as the phone rang, visions of not being able to reach the dealer flashed through my head. I was terrified to have come this close to no avail. I could taste the effects of the drugs already, the adrenalin shot through my body as I envisioned the poison coursing through my veins and lungs.

A gruff voice interrupted me from my day dreaming. I identified myself and immediately started to use some of the code I knew was required when on a phone. "Hey it's me, do you know anyone that needs some smokes?" I asked. "I might" he replied. Pure joy resonated through my body. Up to this point I wasn't sure he was willing to make a deal or perhaps, heaven forbid, he was too busy.

"Well if it isn't too hard for you to get up to the northwest, did you want to hang around for a couple of hours?" I asked. I had used the standard code to tell him where I was, tell him how much I wanted and what it is I wanted.

By saying a couple of hours I had told him I wanted two grams. When I asked "If it isn't too hard for you to get to the northwest" I had told him I wanted crack by saying "hard".

"Yeah, fine" he said "Call me back in twenty."

The deal was struck. What more could I need? I thought. Only moments ago I was despairing over when my next hit would be and here I was perhaps only half an hour away from getting what I truly wanted. After all, I wanted no part of recovery. I wanted to get high.

I signed out and we called a cab. Within minutes we were heading to a local store to get the provisions we needed, needles, cigarettes and vinegar. I had known that asking for powder or cocaine was going to be pointless as this dealer only carried crack and so both Peter and I knew that we would have to alter the drug to be able to inject it.

Like most street drugs you never really know what you are getting, yet there was no hesitation when presented with an opportunity to use. The drug could be cut with almost anything. One method was to cut it with rat poison. Later I would meet people who had permanent scars all over their body from injecting drugs mixed with the rat poison, some had terrible seizures and some I heard about had died.

Yet none of these potential consequences entered my mind as we raced off to score.

We rented a hotel room using Peter's credit card, well within eyesight of the center. Although it was only a little while later, it seemed like hours before I had re-contacted the dealer and arranged a meeting close to the hotel.

Knowing this dealer would snap on me and possibly kill me or even worse not do the deal I knew I couldn't take Peter to the actual buy. So I met the dealer, I had cartons of cigarettes in hand and soon the deal was done.

I could barely sit still in the cab as we drove back to the hotel where Peter waited. I think I was so high from the adrenalin by this point that I was slurring my words. The thoughts of simply going somewhere else alone with the drugs occurred to me several times yet for some reason I still cannot explain, I decided not to rip Peter off.

Upon arriving at the hotel I sprinted up the stairs to the room and immediately started to prepare. Only a few minutes after that Peter and I were each lying on our own bed, head spinning as the poison worked through our systems.

As always happens, soon the drugs wore out. It was now six AM and we had been going hard for about seven hours. When I was using there was seldom any breaks between shots or hits on the pipe. It was always a race to get as much of the drug into myself as fast as possible and as I learned it was the same with Peter. After restocking from the dealer a couple of times throughout the night we wound up using well over six or seven grams.

I tell you the amount and the time it took us to do it, not to try and show how cool we were by the amount we used, but rather to demonstrate how the disease takes hold, how even knowing that this amount may cause us to overdose we were only interested in its consumption.

When the next morning found us we were strung out and already experiencing some of the panic associated with the impending withdrawal. Knowing we could not return to the detox center so quickly I was at a loss as to what to do. I couldn't fathom it when Peter told me he didn't want to charge anymore on his card. I would be lying if I told you I didn't think of simply taking the card from him by whatever means necessary.

What really surprised me was when Peter told me that he had to go downtown. He had an appointment to try and get into a rehabilitation center and since he was homeless he had to get in.

With nowhere else to go, I accompanied him downtown. I waited in a local coffee shop. I hung out with alcoholics and street people, and whiled away the time. After a couple of hours Peter returned and announced that they didn't know he was still high and he was accepted.

Previously we had decided that maybe we might in fact get more drugs and return to the hotel if things didn't go well for Peter at his appointment. However Peter wanted to give this a shot and was already feeling bad about the financial costs of the night before.

As such he told me that he wouldn't be able to use his credit card to get more. How incredibly selfish I thought. Here he was making up some lame story about wanting to get clean and leaving me without access to more drugs.

After a few moments of laying a guilt trip on Peter, never once considering the fact that he might have a real opportunity to do something for himself through this treatment center or the fact that he needed to get off the street; Peter finally gave me his last twenty dollars and escorted me to a well-known area for buying crack.

I bought a "twenty piece" and Peter and I parted ways.

Quite sometime later I ran into Peter again. He told me he was doing well and was getting a hang of this recovery thing. I never saw him again and do not know whatever became of him.

I took my new best friend, the piece of crack, and awaited a bus to take me to my parents' house. After all I had nowhere else to go. In the ten minutes it took for the bus to arrive I had already used the drugs. Even though by now it was broad daylight and downtown was filled with people leading their lives and going to work I used right there at the bus stop in plain sight. I had no regard for the fact this action may get me arrested nor did I care what those around me thought.

It had been hours since my last hit and I wanted it now.

My parents knew I was going into the detox center and was not supposed to be out yet, so my mother was surprised when I entered. I made up some lame story about how I was allowed to leave early. Even knowing at the time my mother didn't believe me I was now only fixated on the horror of the impending withdrawal.

It was then my mother told me that Susan had tried to contact the center where I was supposed to be in an attempt to allow me to say goodbye to my son. She was leaving for Vancouver and I had just blown my opportunity to say goodbye to the one person I thought I cared for.

While I was getting high in a hotel room with a stranger, injecting unknown substances into my veins and flirting with death, my son was already on the road heading to the coast.

Chapter 18

"A Moment Of Clarity"

I had become dead inside. I thought that I was above all of the emotional issues associated with life. My son was now living with his mother on the coast. I had almost destroyed all the relationships that I once held dear and yet I lied to myself and thought that I was without regret.

Life by this point had become nothing more than an inconvenience.

I clearly remember injecting myself and wondering if the amount I had just done would kill me. When it didn't there was a very clear feeling of disappointment and an immediate need to do more.

I had started the thirty second year of my life still in possession of those things that I now long for. I had a newborn son, a marriage, a house and a job that in itself provided an opportunity for success and monetary gain.

Now I stood in front of a homeless shelter. I had just recently been kicked out of my parents' house yet again and had been sheltered for a few days by a friend who no longer used.

It was a cold night in the middle of November and I was alone and totally oblivious to the fact that it was my actions that had brought me to this point.

While walking to the shelter I had been offered drugs by several street corner dealers and I felt regret that I had no money to take advantage of their wares.

Drugs had led me to this point and I was disappointed I couldn't afford to purchase more.

So there I stood in line waiting to find shelter for the evening; my prize possessions were two empty syringes and a spoon. If any good came of this moment it was a lasting realization of what is important in life. To me it isn't the amount of money in the bank or the type of vehicle you are driving; it is family, serenity and the sense of hope.

At this exact moment none of these things held any importance to me. I was only concerned with the most standard things that I used to take for granted like a roof over my head and where my next meal was coming from.

I had become exactly what I used to look down my nose at. Drugs had brought me to my knees and yet I was unwilling to take a hard look at my nemesis.

I entered the shelter and was taken aback by the sheer number of those of us seeking help. Hundreds of people lined the walls. Their biggest aim in life at the moment was the desire for somewhere to lay their head.

Here I found humanity at its best and its worst; for all around me people suffered and toiled through everyday life and while they were lost in their addictions, mental issues or had trouble overcoming a bad hand they had been dealt in life, there were those who worked there and were offering what help they could.

The stereotypes had been cast aside and the only goal was to offer assistance where they could.

Regardless of the fact there were so many people around me in the exact same predicament, I still found that I felt alone. For some reason I could not look past my own plight and difficulties and come to the understanding that we all shared the same types of difficulties.

Here I was no different, no better and no worse than those I stood in line with yet somehow I managed to kid myself that for some inexplicable reason I was superior. Perhaps I still felt that I was truly unique in my situation. After all how could anyone else endure the pain and difficulty I was experiencing?

In spite of the glaring examples all around me I still was blind to the fact I was not alone.

Lunacy once again reared its head and I decided that as soon as I could I would obtain more drugs and find shelter in their intoxicating effect. Certainly that would show everyone! No matter how much they wanted to control me I thought I would show them. I would use again.

I had grown accustomed to the necessity of watching my back and being aware of those around me. This was only about survival. Humanity had been reduced to its most basic function and other than being on the street this was never more evident to me than the situation I was in.

Little did I know at the time that through the perception of having to be tough and untouchable I was only serving to heighten the walls I was building against others. Through this mind set I was only serving to further distance myself from the love and help those around me had once offered.

Through my actions and attitudes to ensure my survival in this type of setting I was also limiting the possibility of accepting the help I would need to endure. By attempting to live, I was eliminating the possibility of that survival.

As I stood in line behind so many other lost souls, an offer came from one of the people working to lay out some of the mats that people would be sleeping on. Luckily for me I accepted and was put to work. Had I not, instead of a bed, I would have joined hundreds of others attempting to sleep on the floor mere inches from someone they didn't know.

When it came to finding a place to sleep ideals like security, comfort and privacy were quickly cast aside.

I was told to wear the gloves offered; although the mats were washed daily there was still a chance that unknown substances and possible disease were left on the cushions that people would be sleeping on that very night.

Since I had helped I was given a bed on one of the upper floors. Although basic at best the accommodations were still better than those found downstairs and I was afforded the comfort of a pillow and a sheet.

Unfortunately I was still going through withdrawal from my latest usage; this in combination that truthfully I was scared. I was worried about being attacked during the night and that meant that I couldn't fall asleep and soon found myself wandering the halls.

Several staff informed me that the bed was for people that wanted to sleep however if I truly felt I couldn't sleep I could go into the smoking area and remain quiet so as to not disturb those that so desperately needed their rest.

I walked into the haze filled room and found several others with the same difficulty in sleeping as I had. Soon I was engaged in conversation with Bill. I didn't know it at the time but Bill was an example of who I would become if I didn't seek help and soon.

Bill had been on the streets since the age of 14 and was fully immersed in any criminal activity he could find to sustain his addiction. Soon the conversation turned to the need to procure more drugs and how great they were.

Together we reveled in the thoughts associated with each intake of the poisons we used to drown out the voices of despair. Somehow we fed off each other's addiction and together we rejoiced in the depravity of the disease.

Bill explained to me how he had several associates who were also living at this shelter; that is when they could get a bed. He detailed their illegal activities and after ensuring I was not a cop he invited me to join them in their escapades.

It had taken me less than 12 hours to go from a friend's couch to the chance to yet again associate with those that would further enable my using.

At this point I did not care for the fact that it was obvious that in joining them I would continue to sink lower. I knew that the activities they were proposing to me would only lead to death or jail and yet that realization paled in comparison to the idea that they would help me secure more drugs.

After all what did I need with family, friends, security and peace when I could simply block my internal desire for these things with the use of drugs?

Even through all of this the internal battle raged. There were still parts of me that wanted something better, a new life, a new beginning and so I removed myself for a while from Bill and his love of "the life."

Once again making my way through the upper floor of the shelter I ran into an addiction's counselor who worked there. She knew immediately where I was at and for one moment of clarity I sought help. I asked about the rehabilitation program I had heard of that the shelter offered.

To this day I do not think she believed I was ready and yet she took the time to explain the steps I would have to take to gain entrance into the program.

With great hesitation I turned over the needles I carried and the spoon I cherished. Perhaps knowing this may be a critical step for me she smiled and agreed to dispose of them.

We stood in silence for a while, the internal battle raging. Unfortunately for me at that exact moment the call of the drugs and the desire to revel in the chaos they brought won out.

I can still vividly remember her smile turning from one of hope to sadness as she saw in my eyes the decision I had come to.

I thanked her for her time and returned to Bill.

Things will be different tomorrow I lied to myself. Certainly I could get that type of help whenever I chose to. Wouldn't it always be there for me? Regardless of the fact that I now spoke to a person who had been lost in his addiction for almost a decade; in spite of the examples of how lost you can get in this disease and even knowing it can get a lot worse I kidded myself into thinking that somehow I was still in control.

Without warning the new day's sun burst through the windows. I have seen many sunrises since and still the difference in the message they brought could not be any different in what I perceived this day. With the sun's rising I saw myself giving over and giving up.

Instead of taking advantage of the help so readily available I had resigned myself at this point to a life of crime; a life of no higher purpose that the pursuit of finding and using drugs.

Soon after Bill and I were told it was time to clean our beds and make our way downstairs for breakfast. Upon arriving I was soon introduced to the four other members of this group who had managed to find room in the shelter for the evening.

Perhaps it was my obvious desperation or the fact those mere moments ago I had given up but I was quickly accepted and soon the talk turned to planning the day.

I wish I could find a more eloquent way to describe what happened to me next. Upon reflecting on it, to try and find flowery words would minimize how effective the miracle about to happen was. It finally reached that portion of me that still wanted to live.

It was as if at this precise moment God slapped me upside the head.

I heard no angel's voice. I had no visions that inspired me to reach higher in my goals. There were no trumpets playing yet with incredible clarity I suddenly saw what lay in store for me. At that moment the fact that I had a choice had never been so clear.

Before me I saw two roads; one that led to the inevitable death that I sought or one that, although filled with difficulties in overcoming the damage I had brought, also led to redemption.

I recall coming out of a fog with one of the guys calling me repeatedly. It was if I had left my body for a moment. I had been shown what lay in store and a quiet voice had asked me to choose.

"You know what guys": I asked, "I think I am going to call the detox center and see if I can get in."

The reaction of those, those mere moments ago, I was so ready to cast my fate with was no more sorrowful than if someone had told them that we were having Rice Krispies instead of corn flakes.

My lack of desire to follow them would in no way deter them from what they had planned for the day. Whether I was there or not they would continue on their chosen path and if I wanted to go another way, so long as I didn't get in their way, they couldn't care less.

With that I left the table walked over to the free telephone and called my brother. "I think I need help" I said when he answered. "I think maybe I should try going to the detox center again."

Remembering now his reaction still brings tears to my eyes. I do not think I could hold it against him if he'd said "You know what I have heard this before, find your own way to the center." Yet he didn't.

In a quiet and yet supportive voice he simply said "Where are you? I'll come get you."

Within half an hour I had been offered a choice, shown what lay in store for me either route I took and had been saved from the cusp of hell by a family member that just last night I was willing to try and forget about.

Without regard for personal safety my brother came into one of the more dangerous areas of town and soon I was on route to make what I could of yet another chance I had received.

This time, I thought, things will be different.

Chapter 19

"Rehab"

I stood out in front of the rehabilitation center and to me it looked far more like a prison than a place to find a solution. Before me I only saw a place where I would be stripped of all the excuses I had used to continue my life of using.

Up to now I had felt completely justified in the way I was living my life. After all, as I have said many times before, I thought if anyone had to endure what I had to go through then they would use as well.

However, deep down I knew that these were simply lame excuses I was telling myself to try and justify my behavior. I therefore did not envision the treatment center as a place of recovery but simply as something that would jeopardize my using.

Somehow I had managed to get my name on the waiting list for this place while white knuckling it after having left the detox center. In fact it was an ex-employee who had also been through this place that recommended it to me.

Originally I had put my name on the list just so I could once again get people off my back. I had felt that so long as I had this outward sign of wanting to get clean no one could fault me if I used in the interim.

With great trepidation I entered the center. My parents were so completely supportive that they drove me the nine hour trip it had taken to get to this place in another province.

I was so incredibly scared of what lay in store for me, so completely convinced was I that I had nothing to offer. I was truly fearful that by going through treatment I would be stripped of all the things that had sustained me for so long.

For as long as I could remember I had fed off of my own fear and insecurities; and so I had grown accustomed to the negativity associated with that mental state I thought that if that mind set was removed what would I have left?

If all that was wrong in my thinking and actions was to be removed, what would happen if I didn't like what was left? What would happen if I found out who I truly was and didn't like what I saw?

My biggest fear was that of the unknown. I hated the idea of change.

Once again the thought of being alone in my predicament was first and foremost; yet something gave me the power to walk into the center. Something guided my steps when I couldn't find the strength to do it on my own.

Upon reflecting on this previously, I had convinced myself that it was simply the fact that if I didn't go I would be stranded in another province. I would be miles from home without any ability to sustain myself.

In truth now I know that it was God helping me to do what I could not do on my own.

Being so fearful I once again resorted to my standard attitude of being untouchable by both emotion and the influence of others and so with this attitude I walked in and was greeted by the staff.

Immediately I was given the impression that the normal attitudes of the street and the life of a using drug addict would not be tolerated. I was told to tell my parents to wait before leaving because even now there was no certainty that I would be accepted.

Regardless of the distance traveled I would have to go through an induction process and only then would my eligibility be determined.

After a lengthy interview process that included hammering the rules of the center into my brain, an inspection of my luggage to ensure

I hadn't brought any drugs with me and a visual inspection of my arms, legs and feet to ensure I hadn't used recently was I accepted.

Going into the facility I had eighteen days clean. Somehow I had managed to maintain sobriety for what seemed like an eternity at this point and was eligible to gain access.

Part of me, a very large part in fact, truly wished I wouldn't be accepted and I could use that as yet another excuse to continue using.

Well I tried to go to rehab and it's not my fault they didn't accept me. What more can you ask of me, I thought?

Yet I was unable to use this excuse as, after much time, I was told I would be given a room and entered into the program. At the time it just seemed as if another door had closed behind me.

I started to feel like a caged animal and the desire to run, run anywhere but where I was at started to consume me.

Regardless of how fearful I was, I held it in as I bid my parents farewell. I could tell how proud of me they were. How ready they were to forgive and forget all that had led up to this moment; however this attitude of acceptance they held only angered me.

After all I did not want to be forgiven. I was, in my mind, the worst there ever was. Never before had an addict done the things I had. No one in the history of man had sunk so low and so I viewed myself as being beyond forgiveness.

At the end of the day my ability to view myself as being so incredibly unique and without merit is what sustained me and gave me the ultimate excuse to use and so when others would not buy into this thought process of self-pity it truly angered me.

Didn't they know who I was after all? Were they truly blind to all the things I had done? Could they not understand I was completely justified in my using and lifestyle?

Shortly thereafter I was given a tour of the facility and shown to my room. At the time I can recall how happy I was that I was given a private room and did not have to share with someone else. Even then I was so convinced I was superior to anyone else going through rehab that I didn't consider myself as one who had to lower themselves to having to share a room.

Little did I know that this mind set would only serve to continue to isolate me and make me even more resistant to the changes I needed to make.

There was no time for further reflection as I was thrust into the normal day to day of being in rehab. After being shown to my room I was introduced to my counselor, shown the ropes of the center and put to work.

I was told there would be no time to sit around and feel sorry for myself and that if I did not toe the line I would be asked to leave.

Little time was spent on an attitude of not wanting to be there. That was a given. Very few of us truly wanted to be there and so given that this was simply accepted; acting distant or unwilling to cooperate in my own recovery was simply not tolerated.

After all, I was told, if I didn't become active in my recovery there were others literally dying to get in. The true reality of this statement and how closely this thought process was followed wouldn't become apparent until later in my treatment when I witnessed those who faced a return to jail or life back on the street being asked to leave because they were not willing to do the work.

At the time I couldn't believe how callous this was. How could you kick someone out who almost certainly faced death or being in jail? It wouldn't be until much later I would learn that you had to be willing to put in the effort and truly want recovery before you were able to be helped.

Although I thought the passage of time was incredibly slow, soon the days started to run together as slowly my defenses were broken down.

We had a very strict daily routine that was to be followed without question. I can often remember thinking this was no better than jail. I viewed these restrictions as a removal of my self will and an encroachment upon my rights. Little did I know at the time that the structure being taught was exactly what I needed.

I was so used to setting my own course in life and following my own will that I didn't realize that eliminating this self-destructive pattern was the only way in which I would eventually be open to the changes I needed to make.

There seemed to be no end to the work we were required to do. We received little in the way of down town and so our days were filled with traipsing from one scheduled activity to another.

It is funny to me now how much I resisted the change and yet how predictable my actions and thoughts were to those that staffed the center. It was inexplicable to me at the time how they knew, often before I did what my next attitude was going to be.

As I had done so often in my life I attempted to close down emotionally, to put up the walls that I thought protected me but only served to keep me in my negative state.

The worst for me was the smaller counseling sessions we received twice a day. Here I was asked by my counselor George to face those demons I had carried for so long. Without fail I was expected to share my emotional state and to truly delve into the issues that had prolonged my using.

I was not asked, so much as told, to daily reflect on the events and the emotional baggage I carried to justify my using. In depth George told me I had to examine these events, especially the ones that surrounded my separation from my son and failed marriage.

As the emotional walls I had created started to show signs of wearing down I could not believe the pain that lay behind them. I was subjected to such emotional turmoil that often I tried to crawl back into myself seeking refuge from what I perceived to be intolerable pain.

As George made abundantly clear by sharing his own experiences we were not alone in our depravity. Addiction was a problem that many shared and we were not as unique as we had thought.

In fact, as it turned out, George was even familiar with some of my own haunts having spent time in the same city as I.

I was forced to face all that had held me back, all that I had done and even worse I had to accept responsibility for the part I played in all of these events.

Slowly I started to realize I was not the victim I had thought I was and that I had in fact played a significant role in where I was.

I think one of the most important lessons I learned while going through treatment, was that addiction is a disease. It is not, as I had mistakenly perceived, a fault of character or a lack of self will.

I was not less because I was an addict. I would not turn my nose up at someone who had cancer so why would I feel less because I too suffered from a disease.

In fact I should feel lucky that if one had to have a disease was it not better to be inflicted with one that is treatable.

There are many life threatening diseases and many find when they are diagnosed there is nothing that can be done; yet here I was learning that the disease I carried had, if not a cure, at least a way to treat it.

In addition I learned that I was not alone. Many before me had found a way to face the challenges of everyday life and in fact had overcome the damage they had caused while using. They had learned to not simply use those transgressions and initial inability to deal with day to day life as an excuse to use.

After a while I started to settle into the center and actually find hope. I started to look forward to the counseling sessions as a way to learn a better way. I would be lying however if I said it was always a learning experience I took full advantage of.

Almost hourly it seemed I fought an internal battle to make the most of this opportunity. All too often it seemed I would slip back into my old defenses. I would resort to sarcasm to defend against the onslaught of emotions I faced. As the work we did and the counseling George provided attempted to delve deeper into the emotional state I was in, I found myself making snide remarks and closing my mind to the help being offered.

What finally started to set in was that this attitude and reluctance to let go of some of these self-imposed restraints would not be tolerated. It was once again made abundantly clear to me that I was fully expected to do the work when I witnessed one of the others in my group threw a hissy fit in treatment.

Since entering into treatment only a week after I had, Cory had held onto the belief that perhaps he didn't need treatment. He often complained about how unique he was in his problems and that no one knew the pain he carried.

The fact that this so clearly demonstrated my own mind set and how potentially dangerous this thinking was, really struck home when one day during one of our sessions Cory lashed out at those of us in the group including George. "I have had enough" he yelled "I don't have to take this" and with that he stormed out, returned to his room and began to pack.

Even then I knew Cory was truly taking his life into his own hands. I was fully aware by this point how we now faced a choice between life and death and yet here Cory was throwing away the opportunity that lay before him.

With great reluctance George decided to follow Cory down to his room and there they apparently had a little chat. After some time George returned to the counseling session and informed us that Cory had asked to stay. George told us that he had informed Cory that his attitude and behavior was not acceptable and was told that the answer was no. He had to go.

I must admit that it took me some time to realize how correct was the decision to let him go. Slowly I figured out that Cory was not only jeopardizing his own life but that of those around him.

His negative attitudes were poison to the rest of us. Although many of us often shared his mind set, at least the majority of the people in our group, by this point, were willing to try and work on a better way.

By allowing Cory to stay he could potentially have turned our attention away from the help offered. Given our tenuous state, it would be all too easy to push us towards the destructive lifestyle we had been living.

With this lesson in mind I set myself to get as much as possible out of my time at the center. I earnestly turned my attention to the daily exercises and probably for the first time after entering rehab, put my best effort into recovery.

Over the next couple of weeks I was introduced to a twelve step program. Little did I know at the time that this would eventually help to save my life.

After a while my time at the center came to a close and regardless of what I had learned I still perceived my leaving the center as being released from prison.

However I had a new attitude. Once again the chance at a new way of living seemed promising. No longer did I perceive my life as potentially being filled with despair.

The problem though was I made a huge mistake. I envisioned myself as cured. I mistakenly thought that now that I had put this effort into my recovery I was done.

It would not be long after leaving treatment that I would learn how potentially fatal this mind set could be.

Chapter 20

"Bottom At Last"

I had returned from the rehabilitation center full of hope and with an eye to the future. Already I was planning my new life and how I was going to carry it out. Unfortunately the lessons of having to continue to work at recovery didn't take hold.

When I came back home I thought I was cured. Sure I could go to a twelve step meeting but wasn't that for people who hadn't been to treatment?

In retrospect I can see now that it only took me a few weeks to learn how vital that lesson was. Sitting in my parents' basement I took a phone call. A voice on the other line identified herself as a nurse for the region's health facility.

Prior to going into treatment I was asked to get a blood test; since I never heard back from any doctor regarding the test I assumed all was well.

The nurse had other news however and quickly informed me that I had Hepatitis C.

At the time I knew nothing about the disease; however it was not long before I learned all there was to know.

It took some time before I was seen at the local Hepatitis clinic and informed about the potential effects. According to the doctor, I had the first of six different genotypes of the virus and unfortunately this was the one that could cause the most damage.

Shortly thereafter I was given a liver biopsy and informed that out of a range of one to four my liver was at a stage two for both swelling and scarring.

Apparently it is the scarring that can lead to cancer and that, in combination with the potential liver failure, made treatment the only potential solution.

Even now I am amazed at my reaction. Even while facing the possibility of the disease getting out of control I was almost happy that once again I had an excuse. In all honesty I don't think that at that time I wanted to be cured.

I wanted an excuse to continue using and truth be told I think I still wanted to die. In short I didn't want the treatment to work.

Regardless of the glimmer of hope I had obtained by going to a rehabilitation center I had still not found a meaning. I had looked inside myself and been repulsed. I wanted to die.

Although I agreed to the treatment, secretly I wanted nothing to do with the potential healing it offered; and so regardless of rehab and the occasional twelve step meeting, it was not long before I was out and using again.

I remember distinctly the first time I called the dealer after rehab. I recall how the rush of adrenalin was so great that I could barely walk. On route to meet the dealer I was ecstatic.

On the way I stopped at a drug store and equipped myself with some syringes. Walking over to meet him took an eternity. I was full of fear, not that I was about to use again but rather that I might miss him or that he wouldn't show up.

Minutes seemed to last an eternity as I waited outside a local bar for his arrival. Finally he showed up and the deal was made.

I didn't even wait to get back home; I immediately went into the bar's bathroom and shot up.

It was like coming home, all of my fears and insecurities left me as I sat back and let the rush wash over me. I no longer cared about how

I had blown the little amount of sobriety I had. The concerns over my health were a thing of the past.

Once again I was high and this, I thought, was not only what I was comfortable with but also no more than I could expect. Hadn't I simply been fooling myself? After all who was I kidding? I had sacrificed everything for drugs, I had long ago sold my soul for this life and to think I could now escape was lunacy.

Soon after this I started treatment for the Hepatitis. Little did I know at the time how much the side effects of this treatment would rule my life. Each day I took six pills and once a week I had to inject myself.

The procedure for getting the needle ready for the treatment was much the same as when I was shooting up. I would mix the provided saline with the drug, which was a white powder and then inject myself.

Even when I was trying not to use drugs this procedure often triggered a desire to use. The blood tests that I frequently had to have did much the same. By this time a lot of my veins had collapsed and it was very difficult for the nurse to find one. After quite some time of her digging around she would finally hit.

I remember how excited I would get as she drew back on the plunger and I saw the blood enter the needle. I sat expectantly awaiting the rush I associated with this and was always disappointed when, of course, nothing happened.

My treatment for Hepatitis C was to last 48 weeks. This was a long time of being constantly sick, entire body rashes and a real problem with both depression and sleep.

Eventually my thyroid started to shut down and this added to the difficulties I experienced.

Although I was trading a potentially life threatening disease for a lifelong treatable condition the damage to my thyroid was just one of many significant problems I faced as a result of the treatment for Hepatitis C.

I had long been depressed and as a direct result of the treatment this depression deepened. In fact it is standard to put patients on an anti-depressant because of this side effect.

For almost a year I felt as if I had the flu. I was often sick to my stomach, my muscles ached constantly and more often than not I ran a fever.

At times the side effects were so significant I often considered simply stopping the treatment even knowing that this decision could lead to a liver failure or even death.

By this time I was receiving disability and so once a month I would get my check in the mail and immediately run down to the closest bank. As soon as I had the cash in my hand I would meet a dealer and buy as much drugs as I could.

I no longer had a bank account since all my accounts had been closed. By this time I was over $100,000.00 in debt.

This continued on for some time. My life became a cycle of using, white knuckling it until my next check came and then starting the whole process over again. Occasionally I would reach out for help, usually though only after having run out of drugs.

Every once in a while I would speak to George from the treatment center I had attended. He would try his best to point me in the right direction, reminding me of the lessons I had learned in treatment; however without fail I would wind up using again.

Things were not all bad at this point though, as my communication with Susan has started to increase and through that I was getting more opportunities to speak to my son.

More often than not I would lie awake at night refusing to allow the tears that filled my eyes to run down my face. Being away from my son left a hole in my heart and regardless of the amount of drugs I used I could never fill it.

Of course I lied to everyone around me that I was clean and had been since treatment. Once again dishonesty had simply become another thing I accepted and lived by.

Through our many conversations Susan and I started to discuss attempting to reconcile and I was astonished that a really possibility of being with my son was there. In truth I had long ago given up on my marriage and honestly can't say I was interested in getting back together with Susan.

Yet here was a chance to be with my kid again and if that meant faking an interest in repairing our marriage I was willing to do it.

Before long my dream came true and I flew out to stay with Susan.

I recall seeing my son for the first time in a great while at the airport. He and his mother were walking down the sidewalk when she pointed me out to him. "Look there's Daddy" she said.

He took one look at me and began running towards me, his little legs pumping for all they were worth, his arms outstretched. There was no judgment on his face, no apparent recollection of bad times just an unconditional love. He held a true desire to be with his father and so he jumped into my arms.

This was heaven! Holding my boy close to me, so tightly in fact, that I could feel his heart beating in time with my own. I couldn't recall a time when I had ever felt so complete, so accepted or so loved.

Susan's parents still held a hatred for me, believing that I had ruined her life and so they were not informed that I was back.

As such I would stay with Susan and my son until they came into town at which time I would have to fly back to Calgary.

Whenever I left I wouldn't know when, or even if, I would return. Each time was a heart breaking experience saying goodbye to my little boy at the airport. Every time I was haunted on the way home by the look in his eyes; questioning why his daddy was leaving.

He was too young to understand and I couldn't explain it to him. I had thought that I had experienced all the sadness one could feel up until now yet every time I left the breaking of my heart took me to another low.

I would return home cash in hand and wouldn't even make it out of the terminal before I was on the phone making arrangements to pick up more drugs. Whenever I was around my son, I wouldn't use. I remained clean so that I could be a father. However, when I left that inspiration went, and I would inevitably get high.

This cycle led to me finally hitting bottom.

One night while using I suffered the worse seizure and psychosis I ever had. I was once again in my parent's basement shooting up. I had filled the syringe with as much as I could get into it and my last coherent memory before the seizure was that of me injecting.

All I can recall is flashes of fear that I was being attacked by my eldest brother and throwing wild punches at him.

What actually happened is that I dropped in the bathroom and began thrashing. My brother was called over and attempted to restrain me as I thrashed about. The seizure was so violent that I kicked the toilet off of its base and kicked down the shower stall. I still to this day have the scars on my foot from that.

When I came to I was in a bedroom surrounded by paramedics and police. I was in a state of confusion and didn't know what had happened.

After much convincing by all of the emergency staff I was once again taken to the hospital. After all that I had been through; after all of the near death experiences; my exposure to violence and the way I had given everything away for drugs and the life that comes with it, what amazes me is what finally hit home.

As the paramedics wheeled me into the hospital we passed by a smaller room for those with mental problems who had become violent. As I looked into the window on the door I saw a woman, her face pressed against the glass. I was immediately taken aback by the way she looked out with no expression on her face. Her eyes were dead and she seemed to have no reactions to being locked in this room as if she truly didn't know where she was.

I was horrified at the realization that if I continued on the path I was on, I too would wind up in a room such as this. It seemed that at the time I still didn't fear death but rather winding up permanently in a state of psychosis.

Given the events of the evening I finally found the bottom of my downward spiral into the hell the life of an active drug user takes on.

After several hours of being monitored I was released. The doctor, having read my medical chart and realizing how many times I had been there for the exact same thing, had little patience with me.

I returned to my parents' house wondering what their reaction was going to be. I fully expected to once again be kicked out and so with great trepidation I walked in.

Upon entering I found both of my parents waiting up for me regardless of the late hour. I could see the hurt and frustration in their eyes. Lamely I apologized for once again using.

I imagine they were surprised I so easily admitted that I had used and were caught off guard by my new honesty. Quietly my mother told me to go downstairs and get some sleep.

I had been given a chance by both my parents and God because yet again I should have probably been asked to leave the house and most assuredly should have died given the amount I used.

Soon after I returned to be with my son once again

Upon returning to Vancouver I contacted George. I told him what had happened and for the first time, maybe ever, I admitted I was scared. "Of course you are" he said "do you think maybe it's time to actually start working on your recovery?" he asked.

"Do you attend a twelve step meeting? Do you have a sponsor? Do you have a home group? Are you working the steps?" He grilled me.

Of course all I could reply was "No."

"Well perhaps you might want to try that."

By this point I was truly desperate and so I did as was suggested. Within a couple of weeks I had done almost everything that was suggested by George and I actually started to accumulate some clean time.

Bruce also lived in Vancouver and without hesitation he made me part of his life. Even through all of the difficulties Susan and I had in our attempt to reconcile, Bruce was always there with a sympathetic ear.

Without hesitation Bruce always stepped up and did as he thought best. He would be a friend and in fact turned out to be the best friend I had ever had.

It is safe to say that through Bruce I learned what friendship truly was.

Every day I was rewarded by the presence of my son and for the first time in quite a while things started to look promising.

I was astounded by the little things. Now the highlights of my day were things like my son waking me up in the morning and crawling into bed with me or holding my hand as we walked somewhere.

Hours spent lying on the floor playing cars or curled up together watching some of his favorite cartoons. Each night I would read a story to him making silly faces and voices and laughing along with him as he laid there wide eyed listening to my renditions of the books he enjoyed.

This is what life was about and through his unconditional love I found the ability to start to love myself.

My time at a local twelve step group was equally rewarding as I found others who could understand my pain. I found a sponsor who could relate and help me though the difficulties of life.

The ultimate test of what I had learned in this short time of recovery was yet to come.

Chapter 21

"Testing Sobriety"

It would be a major understatement to say that Susan's and my relationship was rocky at best. It would seem that the transgressions of the past were not easily forgotten. This unease was heightened by the fact that Susan's parents did not know that we were trying to reconcile.

By this point I was heavily involved in my own recovery and truth be told didn't pay enough attention to Susan's needs. I find it hard to explain how I seemed so selfish but to me it was life and death and if living meant that I had to be selfish then that was what I was going to do.

There can be no doubt that this took a toll on our relationship and to be honest, I can't expect I was easy to live with. The medications often left me ill and without energy. Often I was temperamental and could easily switch from anger to depression without any warning. I believe that in conjunction with the Hepatitis C medication this was also a result of my new found sobriety and inability to properly deal with emotions.

Susan lived in constant fear that at any moment a member of Susan's family would show up and ruin everything. I was always caught in the middle. Several times I offered to call them and tell them what was going on, that Susan and I, for the benefit of our son, were trying to repair our relationship.

However Susan was always fearful of the reaction either of us would get to such a proclamation and forbid me to call. I truly worried about the emotional toll this was taking on Susan as every time the phone rang or the doorbell sounded she immediately tensed up; yet regardless of my efforts Susan seemed to prefer to try and live in secrecy.

As such there never really seemed to be an opportunity to focus on us and so we simply fell into a pattern of killing time. It seemed as if her parents finding out were inevitable and so we simply waited.

Completely opposite to Susan's and my deteriorating relationship the one with my son was blossoming. Each day we drew closer to each other. Since I was still on disability, working my way through the arduous task of the Hepatitis C treatment I was able to focus all of my energy and time on that most special relationship.

Daily the numerous pills and especially the weekly injections left me sick most of the time. Even such simple tasks as going for a walk with my son were difficult and even painful as the muscle cramps became worse as the treatment continued.

Never did I doubt who was to blame for the physical condition I found myself in. After all it was through my actions that I had contracted this potentially fatal disease. However I often wished that I were able to be more active with my son. The fact that Susan's and my relationship was sickly, in truth, bothered me little in comparison to my ongoing desire to strengthen my relationship with my son.

There always seemed to be an underlying need to address all the time I had missed with my son. It was a constant desire to seemingly make up for all of the lost opportunities I had forfeited while I was lost in my addiction.

On top of the normal stresses of life I still found myself in a constant battle to avoid the temptation of drug use. Even while I was confronted with some of the miracles available in recovery, such as being with my son again, the temptation was at times almost more than I could bear.

By this point the thought of using had become almost nauseating yet I still found myself, at times, consumed with the obsession. It was as if a veil came over me as I recalled the supposedly fantastic release from my daily responsibilities and obligations. I would have to concentrate on what would inevitably come after, the loss of money, self-esteem and the sobriety I had gained. Most of all it was if the streets were calling me. For some reason it seemed as if life had become boring when compared to the chaos I had lived through.

Certainly I was grateful for this opportunity and so when the desire to return to the life of a drug dealer or user called I was overcome with feelings of guilt and shame. After all how can one question this opportunity and desire such a repugnant life?

Without fail each night I was plagued by using dreams. These dreams were so vivid that at times, in the dream, I would experience much the same rush as if I had used for real. I would wake in a sweat absolutely terrified by the prospect of doing drugs again. The immediate feeling upon waking was that of immense guilt as I was convinced that I had actually used.

I believe one of the most difficult things to grow accustomed to in sobriety was that all of the emotions I had spent a lifetime avoiding and stuffing deep within myself all seemed to come at once. I was ill prepared to deal with the onslaught of emotions that most take for granted. Simple sadness seemed like a lifelong depression; even happiness, so foreign, plagued me simply because I was unaccustomed to it and didn't know how to handle it.

I had but to look at my arms and the awful scars that remained, to be reminded of my past mistakes. These served as a constant reminder and seemed to lend strength to an inner voice that always questioned my ability to remain sober.

This, I believe, is where I received yet another miracle. Through my work in a twelve step program, my family and Bruce I was able to freely discuss the difficulties I faced and was rewarded with a sympathetic ear and a proverbial kick in the butt when I needed it.

To this day I know that I can count myself among the fortunate for having such a strong support group and finding my way to a program that has helped thousands if not millions of addicts. Truly I wonder how many die as a result of not having these tools available to them in their efforts to get or remain clean.

I am constantly amazed at how my family rallied around me as I started to demonstrate a real willingness to remain clean. Who could blame them if they had walked away; yet as the days turned into weeks and then into months of straight time without using, my family proved once again to be the pillar of my support?

How fortunate was I that I had this support group and the clean time under my belt when my world came crashing down around me.

Susan had left to go shopping and so my son and I were watching a hockey game. Admittedly my son was probably far more interested in the bowl of Kraft dinner he was consuming then the actual game; although he seemed to take great joy in joining his father and periodically yelling at the TV whenever his Dad did.

Regardless of whether he truly understood the game he was quick to mimic me, raising his arms in the air and shouting "Yeah!" every time my favorite team scored.

I recall a sensation that this is what life was meant to be, experiencing the simple joys associated with simply being with your family.

Our game was interrupted by the doorbell. Susan had mentioned, before leaving, that a neighbor was going to drop something off at the house and so I was not the least bit hesitant to answer the door.

To my great shock the opening door revealed Susan's sister.

It took several minutes for each of us to catch our breath. I immensely wished I could at that moment turn back the hands of time and not answer the door for I knew what was going to happen as a result of this mistake.

I invited Susan's sister into the house. "I guess we need to talk" I said. Admittedly I was surprised at how quickly she regained her composure as she accepted my invitation. With my son still enthralled with dispersing his food over the table, Susan's sister and I sat down.

Quite bluntly I told her that Susan and I had been attempting to reconcile and had been for some time. I spoke, at some length, about my efforts to remain free of drugs and detailed my involvement in the twelve step program and even gave her an exact time frame associated with how long I had been clean.

I expressed to her that neither Susan nor I had made known the fact I was back in Susan's life since Susan greatly feared the reaction of her family. Susan had often said that her family's automatic reaction would be to cut her off both financially and from any involvement with the family.

To my great surprise Susan's sister seemed empathetic and assured me that both her and her family were the forgiving type and that if someone was truly repentant that they would be willing to back them up.

I couldn't believe my ears. After all her family, and especially her parents, had done to ensure I was removed from Susan's life this seemed too good to be true.

We spoke for a while after that about my concerns over Susan's relationship with her family and how she needed to be supported by them and not ostracized as I thought they were doing.

I did make clear the fact that I was here to stay. Susan and I had discussed several times that we would overcome any difficulties her family presented and that we would remain together. I ensured myself that her sister understood that I was not again going to be separated from my son.

With assurances that she would leave it up to Susan and me to tell her parents she left asking that Susan contact her when she got home.

The sense of relief I felt was overwhelming. I contacted my mother and Bruce telling them both about the great news. I informed them that I had nothing more to fear, for some time I had been plagued by nightmares of being removed from my son and this was apparently an answer to those prayers.

Although Bruce was happy I must admit he was skeptical. He had been witness to the antics of Susan's family, especially the time they had attempted to bribe him in an effort to convince me to sign over the house Susan and I owned, yet he was happy for my sake and hoped this was true.

When Susan got home I sat her down and as calmly as I could I relayed to her the events of the evening. Instantly she was in frenzy. She was sure her family would freak out. After some time I got her calmed down; after all her sister had assured me that her family would be forgiving and supportive.

Immediately Susan attempted to contact her sister but was unable to. This only added to Susan's worry and while she fretted for the next several days I felt secure in the promises her sister had made.

Truly I felt a fool when it all started to unravel.

A few days later Susan's sister finally called her back. I was at a meeting when this happened and so when I returned I came home to a very angry and confused Susan. She shook with rage as she described the conversation that her sister and she had. Apparently I threatened to take Susan and her family to court to try and take our son away from Susan if they so much as complained once that I was back.

Furthermore she went on to describe how I had admitted to her I was not interested in getting back together with Susan and finally convinced Susan I was only interested in two things. Getting sole custody of our son and trying to take Susan's house away from her in a divorce settlement.

I was flabbergasted, I felt such a fool. I had fallen victim to the lies Susan's sister had told me. How could I be so gullible? It is only now that I realize how I believed what I wanted to, contrary to all the evidence that pointed to a different reaction.

What astounded me was the depths of the lies that Susan's sister told her. They seemed almost ridiculous. Even if this weird plan was what I had in fact intended to do why on earth would I have told her sister? It simply didn't make any sense.

Apparently her sister had ended the conversation by telling Susan that she had twenty-four hours to tell her parents or her sister would. Yet another lie her sister told me was revealed.

It took some time for me to convince Susan that her sister was lying and that I had no intention of trying to take her house. I was quite clear that if her family kicked me out I was not going to roll over as I had while using. I explained how important our son was to me and that unlike what I had done a few years back I was not going to just walk away from him this time.

We spoke through the night. Constantly she questioned me about my motives and each time I assured her that I was not going to do as her sister said I would. After quite some time Susan finally declared that regardless of what her parents said she would stand behind the decision to allow me to live there. She commented on how she knew it was important for me to be in the life of my son and she could easily see how much I loved him and how much he liked having me around.

Two days later Susan finally mustered the courage to call her parents. Once again it turned out her sister had lied and had in fact called her parents to tell them what was happening. A fight between Susan and her parents ensued and I must admit that I was impressed that Susan held her ground reinforcing what we had discussed, the importance of having me in our son's life and how much I had changed.

She detailed to them all of my efforts to remain clean and to get my life back on track. As Susan predicted though, her parents reaction was not supportive at all and they did in fact tell her that it was either me or them.

They insisted that if she did not make me leave that they would not have anything to do with her. They told her I had ruined her life and was only there to try and steal our son and her money. Her mother told her that she wished I had died in my drug use and that all I was going to do was leach off of Susan and drag her down.

Susan and I were devastated. My immediate thought was to go out and get high. This was more worry than I thought I could deal with. Regardless of the hell I had been through, using drugs at times like this seemed like a good solution to the panic I felt.

What I did instead was to call on my support group. I freely discussed what had happened and without shame admitted my fear of being separated from my son. Both my family and Bruce had much the same reaction. They implored me to remember what I had learned in my program, to avoid using again as that wouldn't help the situation. They congratulated me on being able to discuss my problems as opposed to stuffing them as I had done so many times before.

I was greatly relieved to know that once again these people were there for me.

Neither of us slept much that night and often our conversation came back to me needing to constantly reassure Susan that her family was completely wrong about my intentions. In return she repeatedly told me that she would stand by what she had told her parents and that she knew it was time she stood up for herself.

I can't say that I was totally confident that Susan would hold true to this, yet I wanted to believe and so I clung to that hope.

However it wasn't even forty eight hours later that all hell broke loose.

It was a Saturday. I don't think I will ever forget. Susan was having a nap, our son and I were playing in the living room when, without warning, the front door opened and in walked both of Susan's parents, her Uncle and Aunt and two of her male cousins.

Immediately I knew this was bad. Apparently her parents had kept a key to the house and I could tell they were here meaning business. Hesitantly I got up from the couch and told them I would go get Susan.

I went upstairs, my heart in my throat, and awoke Susan. Panicking she quickly dressed and followed me downstairs.

Her parents were not interested in talking rationally. Apparently they thought their daughter needed saving and that is exactly what they intended to do. The questioning began. "What the hell is he doing here?" her father grilled Susan.

"He is here for me and our son" she replied meekly.

I had no intention of going down without a fight but was very cognizant of the effect that any yelling, or heaven forbid, physical fighting, would have on an impressionable three year old. I therefore felt trapped and unable to defend myself as I normally would have.

Both Susan and I went into the garage to have a cigarette. I said "Susan, if you don't want them here tell them to leave." She replied "I can't, they're my parents; anyway they won't just leave." Getting frustrated I said "If you tell them to leave and they won't you can call the police."

It was only then that I looked into her eyes and saw what had truly happened. At that moment I knew she had actually called her parents and told them to come and help remove me from the house.

I was on my own and the woman who only a couple of days earlier had told me she would stand by me now was attempting to have me removed from the house. I said "You called them and told them to come didn't you?" "No" she yelled "I did not." I have always been able to tell when Susan was lying to me and this was one of those times.

Instinctively I took a defensive position. I was not going to go quietly and the fear of being thrown out in a city where I knew few people and without any money scared the hell out of me.

It was then that her mother followed us into the garage. I said to her "I would be happy to sit and talk with you. You should know I am clean and have been for some time." I went on to say, "I am here for my son. He deserves to have me in his life and, given my efforts to correct my mistakes I deserve to be in his life as well."

I could tell instantly there was no room for discussion. She had come here with a mission and no amount of reasoning was going to deter her from her goal. "Good for you" she said in a condescending tone.

"Susan come into the house! Sean needs to leave" she ordered. "I won't go anywhere without my son" I replied. Susan walked into the house and I decided to finish my cigarette. I realized my mistake only after her mother slammed the door and I heard the deadbolt slide into place.

I was locked in the garage like an animal.

I was enraged I could not believe how quickly things had gone bad. All I could think about was my son on the other side of the door and my inability to get to him. Luckily for me Susan had left a cordless phone in the garage and I called my family. After several minutes of speaking to my parents they calmed me down to the point where I decided it was not in mine or my son's best interest to kick in the door.

It started to get hot in the garage so I opened the car door, immediately Susan's parents dispatched one of Susan's cousins to stand outside the open door and I was once again infuriated.

Only the thought of my son's horror kept me from lashing out. I hadn't been this angry in a long while. Every so often Susan's parents would open the door and question me.

"So you two have been living in sin" her father said. "No" I replied "The divorce hasn't been finalized" "I don't believe you" he stated. "Well that doesn't change the facts" I shot back.

Periodically I could hear my son playing in the living room oblivious to the fact his father was being kicked out. My heart seemed to break anew every five minutes as I thought with despair of how bad this situation was.

To add insult to injury Susan's mother would open the door and mock me. "Are you going to leave?" she would ask. "No" I would say "My son needs me." "Well I hope you have a nice sleep in the garage" she would say. I knew though that she was trying to provoke me into doing something I could be arrested for and on the advice of my family I did not fall into her trap.

The ongoing mocking went on for five hours. For an unbelievable time I was left in the garage, my belongings were packed and set into the same cell I was in. I was completely powerless since Susan wouldn't back me up. It was her house and if she wouldn't stand up for me there was nothing that legally I could do.

It seemed a constant battle not to break down and cry as the depths of Susan's betrayal sank in.

Finally I was able to get a hold of Bruce. Although I guess the situation I described didn't surprise him he was still outraged and he and his girlfriend sped over to Susan's house.

When Bruce arrived you could tell he meant business; being such a good friend he was angered to the point where it took me several minutes of strong suggestions that he not take things to the next level. Both Susan and her mother stood in the garage as we prepared to leave both wore equally satisfied and condescending smirks on their faces.

It was around one AM when Bruce and his girlfriend showed up. Without so much as being able to say goodbye to my son or to tuck him in, read stories or listen to songs as we normally had been doing I packed my suitcase into Bruce's car and with a heavy heart, tears in my eyes, we left.

Leaving I knew things were never going to be the same. I also knew that through the struggles I was going to face this testing of my sobriety had just started.

Chapter 22

"A New Tomorrow"

As the kilometers between my son and me increased so too did the pain. Within minutes that pain had become almost physical; at times it felt as if a hand was trying to remove my heart from my chest.

In the recent past there had been several times when I had been separated from my son and had not known when I would see him next. On each of these occasions my first instinct was to search for drugs to kill the pain that I believed would consume me.

This time, however, it was different. The craving to return to the drugs to medicate against the pain was still present yet I knew that I had found the tools to withstand the call.

Still as we drew farther and farther away from Susan's house I openly wept. Eventually we arrived at Bruce's apartment. I had no knowledge of where I was going to live nor did I know how I would financially sustain myself.

In circumstances such as these I had previously rolled over and simply walked away from my son. I had used drugs and the excuse of being an addict to try and ease my conscience. It was at this point I resolved to try and move heaven and earth to ensure I would be part of my son's life. I would not desert him as I had done in the past.

With this newfound resolve I gritted my teeth against the pain and vowed to fight for my rights as a father. Still as my mind played through the recent memories of him and of missing tucking him in bed this very night and not knowing when I would be able to tuck him in again, I fell asleep with the tears streaming down my face.

Through this adversity I made a very important decision. Rather than giving into the pain and searching for an easier way out, I had decided to struggle against these new challenges I faced. Somewhere deep down I knew that with the support of those around me and by using the tools I had learned in recovery I would be victorious.

What struck me was the depths of Bruce's friendship. I had made it almost a life's mission to keep my distance from those around me. I believe now that I did this believing that eventually those who loved me would hurt me. Whether it is from a lack of self-worth or an inability to deal with issues such as trust or acceptance, I believed that being hurt in a relationship was inevitable.

Yet here was Bruce offering what assistance he could provide without a seconds hesitation or apparent desire for repayment. Bruce is not rich and so I am sure it was a strain not only financially but also on his blossoming relationship with his girlfriend to expend such energy on my plight; yet that is exactly what he did.

Even his girlfriend Sharon, who I had only known for a few months, never seemed to resent the attention paid to me or the sacrifices she and Bruce had to make. She was always more than willing to lend a hand where possible.

Along with Bruce and Sharon my family stood up and supported me. However beyond providing emotional support there was not much more that they could do.

I awoke the next morning determined to make it through this test. I quickly found a local meeting of a twelve step program and made sure I attended regularly.

Through the program I had come to know a mentor named Bill and with his support I continued to grow in my recovery. Bill stood beside me and added to the strength of my support group.

Being a recovering addict himself, Bill never judged me. He simply listened when I had to vent, offered advice when I asked for it and guided me in my efforts to resist the call of the drugs.

The using dreams came back with a vengeance and I quickly learned that these dreams became more predominant when I had negative emotions.

I knew almost from the moment I left Susan's house that I would have a major decision to make, whether to try and stick it out in Vancouver or return to Calgary. I must admit that the thought of returning to Calgary would seem like a defeat as if I was running back to my family with my tail between my legs. However this wouldn't be the first or I am sure the last, time I would have to swallow my pride and face reality.

The simple fact of the matter was that without employment I couldn't survive. I was worried about returning to a state of desperation and trying to make a living through illegal means; all of which, I am sure, would return me to a life of once again being a slave to drugs.

I made an effort to call my son each and every day. I was concerned about his emotional state having his father suddenly removed from his life. Wanting desperately to see him again I contacted Susan and made my wishes known.

It was then that she informed me that she had filed the order of visitation that had been imposed a few years back in Calgary when I overdosed. It stated that I had to be supervised when with my son. Regardless of the fact I had lived with him for almost a year now and had certainly looked after him by myself on countless occasions she somehow felt it was necessary to have this order filed in British Columbia.

It is hard for me to not believe that this action was suggested by her parents. Given the time that I had spent alone with my son and the fact I could prove I wasn't using drugs, I can to this day see no other reason for their actions but that of vengeance.

It would not be until much later that I would learn that the court had made a significant mistake accepting this out of province order without a hearing on this issue to see if it was valid. Yet since it was accepted I was bound by the provisions it held.

Upon arriving at Susan's it was clear that she had every intention of following the order and so as Bruce and I walked with my son to the park Susan, her aunt and her cousin followed us.

Although her actions infuriated me I tried to focus solely on my son and this time I had with him. We played for quite a long time in the park, Susan and her entourage camped out close to the play area always keeping us in sight.

Sometime later, when my son was becoming tired, we walked back to Susan's house. The pain I was feeling given the knowledge I would once again have to leave him was amplified a thousand times as we approached the house.

My son, holding my hand, said "Come on daddy, let's watch a movie" and tugged on my hand. Tears welled up in my eyes as I tried to explain to him I couldn't "Daddy has to go now little man" I said, trying not to show him my pain.

I could tell he didn't understand. He was but three years old. His daddy had been with him now for almost a year straight and he wanted to once again cuddle on the couch and watch a movie like we had done so many times in the past.

I kneeled in front of him and hugged him close repeating constantly how much his daddy loved him. From the way he clung tightly to me I believe he knew something was amiss and he too repeated his love for me.

Out of the corner of my eye I saw Bruce turn away from the scene playing out before him. The difficulty in seeing this painful interaction between father and son was clearly evident on his face.

Susan and her family members stood close by. There was no sign that this scene had any effect on them whatsoever and as I rose to go to Bruce's car they quickly gathered my son up and escorted him into the house.

Once again the crushing depression threatened to overtake me as we left the neighborhood, but this time was different as I realized that I too held responsibility for the pain now being caused my son. When examining this situation I could easily see the roll that I played. All of this seemed to stem from my active addiction and once again I vowed to do what I could to fix this and never again be the cause of my son's pain through using drugs.

Shortly after the visit I was forced to face the fact that although Bruce was doing his best to support me I had to return to Calgary. Bruce loaned me the money for a ticket and soon I was flying back.

Once again I was reminded of the differences between this return and so many before it; as we arrived in Calgary although the temptation to call the dealer was there, I found the strength to resist. The knowledge that this would not only be detrimental to me, but also those around me, helped me avoid the call of drugs.

I returned home with a plan. There were things I needed to accomplish such as completing the Hepatitis C treatment and declaring bankruptcy. By this point I was approximately one hundred and twenty five thousand dollars in debt and there was no way I was going to be able to dig myself out of that financial hole anytime in the near future.

I also resolved to ensure I found a local twelve step group and to become as active in this new group as I was back in the group in Vancouver.

My father picked me up at the airport and upon arriving back at my parents' house I sat them down and outlined my plan. Upon completion of these tasks I had set out for myself, I was going to return to Vancouver to be close to my son. I had no idea of what job I could get or how in reality I could support myself but I was convinced that I was supposed to go back.

My parents are faithful followers of Christianity and it wasn't long before I started to attend church with them. I must admit that the first time I went with them I was extremely uncomfortable in the house of God.

It felt as if there was a spotlight cast upon me as soon as I walked in. It seemed like everyone was staring at me outraged that I had the audacity to come into this place. I felt like everyone knew of my past misdeeds and forgiveness was not an option.

As the service progressed there were a few people who had been scheduled for baptism. I sat in silence and watched. Instead of seeing people finding God I was simply reminded of the commitment that I had made in the same fashion several years ago, and once again, the feelings of guilt overwhelmed me and in tears I ran from the service.

These feelings of guilt resided with me day and night for several weeks. I attempted to turn in prayer to God yet could not seem to get over the feelings of hypocrisy. It was then that I turned to the pastor of my parent's church who, as it turns out, had had his own difficulties in the past with addiction.

Over the next few days I met several times with the pastor and carefully he guided me through this difficulty. Once again I had found a strong member for my support group. He told me that I had but to talk to God in an honest manner, that God had big shoulders and that he would welcome me back.

I came to the realization that it was not God that had turned his back on me but rather that I had turned my back on him and that he was waiting for me to return.

That night in the quiet of my bedroom, I knelt and was honest with God. I expressed my pain at being away from my son I even told Him of my feelings that He had deserted me and I honestly described my fear.

I was overcome with a sense of comfort and acceptance. It was on this night and through the following months that I found through Him the strength to fight the disease of addiction. I also came to realize that I had worth and I was truly accepted.

Even to this day as thoughts of drug use surface or I am having difficulty dealing with situations and emotions I can find the strength through prayer to overcome these difficulties.

One day I received a call. At first I did not recognize the voice and only after a few minutes of awkward conversation did I realize that the person calling was one of those people I used to buy drugs from.

He informed me that he was changing his phone number, which is common with dealers and he wanted to ensure I had the new number. I would be lying if I said that I wasn't tempted to write down the number or even worse yet ask him to come by my house right away.

However having started to develop the tools required for recovery and the fact I had grown stronger with the help of my support group, I was able to tell him that I didn't want the new number and that I had quitted using drugs.

I could tell he was surprised, yet he said he was proud of me. Although it is impossible for me to believe he was actually happy that he had potentially lost a customer, it is an indication perhaps of how bad things were when your dealer agrees you needed help.

There is no denying that the tests to my sobriety continued as time passed. There were several incidents where I would suddenly be overcome with a feeling of dizziness, my eyelids would flutter, my heart would race and I would break out in a sweat. The most disconcerting thing was that it felt exactly like I had felt when I was about to have a seizure from using too much drugs.

After this happened several times I finally swallowed my fear of the potential answer and consulted my doctor. After a brief visit he confirmed that it was his opinion that I had in some way damaged my brain enough while using that these were in fact minor seizures. However they were not strong enough to require medication. I asked "Will they go away?" In a blunt tone he indicated it was unlikely.

Once again I was faced with fear! In retrospect this seems to be one of the major factors in my drug use; however I was able to overcome this and persevere without medicating myself.

Day by day the indecision as to whether to return to Vancouver plagued me. Each night I would ask God in prayer to help me with this major dilemma.

About a week after I started praying for this I was given the opportunity to speak to a group of youth about my experiences. Now in recovery, I believed that since I was blessed to survive I had a very strong obligation to those who still suffered and if I could, prevent them from following the same path I took. To that end I felt that my calling was to start giving back by becoming an addictions counselor.

With this in mind I jumped at the chance to start making good on this obligation and so I went and spoke honestly to the kids gathered there about the difficulties brought on by drugs.

About a week later I received a phone call from one of the parents that had heard my talk. He informed me there was a camp called Camp Carmangay that held cost-free camps for disadvantaged or troubled teens and that perhaps I might want to volunteer there.

Excited by this chance I called the Camp's owner and introduced myself. Shortly thereafter I met Brian and was impressed by the passion he demonstrated for helping those children who needed help. I told him my story and immediately we hit it off. From what had started as a chance meeting and an attempt to volunteer, I had now been offered a job working with the Camp and those who attended; as well as taking my story into schools.

Through this opportunity I would also have a chance to pursue a degree in addiction counseling.

I didn't miss the fact that God had answered not only my prayers on where I should live but he had provided a way for me to give back. I had no false thoughts that I could save the world yet now I could hopefully pay back the great gift that was given to me.

I had finished my hepatitis C treatment and eagerly awaited the next blood test. As it stands today I have a sixty five percent chance of being cured and will find out more conclusive findings in one month's time.

The side effects of the treatment seem to continue today as I still have low energy and difficulty sleeping. I am now on medication to try and help me recover from the damage did to my thyroid. Even in light of these difficulties they are insignificant when compared to the damage the drugs and the associated life caused me.

My worst day clean is still much superior to my best day while using.

To this day I still have the scars on my arms that remind me of my IV drug use. Yet I no longer see this as something that should cause embarrassment. I even now wear short sleeve shirts not fearful of the reaction of others. I now see these scars as a sign that I have been through a war and so far I am victorious.

I continue to stay in contact with my son. I see him every three days on the webcam but it seems a poor substitute to being able to hold and play with him. I miss the hours we spent playing cars, singing and dancing. I fear that he will look back on this time with regret that his father was not around as much as he would have liked.

When I see him on the internet I make sure to tell him how much I miss and love him.

Recently my parents and I drove out to British Columbia to see him. We spent a weekend together and it was like we were never apart. Although it was extremely painful to leave him at the end of the weekend I cling to the fact that our time together was as comfortable as if we were never apart.

Each day I pray he will not forget me and I vow to continue to fight to be part of his life.

As I write this and come close to the completion of this book I am thirteen days from celebrating my first year clean from drugs. A milestone that not so long ago I thought was impossible; not just difficult to imagine. I don't think that so long ago it was a goal I even wanted.

To reach a year of sobriety will be the longest time I have been clean since the age of 14.

I cannot answer whether I will ever use drugs again. I know not what the future holds however I am convinced that I have a role to play on this earth. My life now has meaning.

I can say that I will not use drugs today and as far as I am concerned that is good enough for now.

A friend once said to me that where there is life there is hope.

Chapter 23

"Closure"

As I sit here contemplating how I am going to end this retelling of my downfall and eventual rebirth in recovery, I am filled with so many emotions they are hard to distinguish.

Most predominantly seems to be bitter-sweet sadness: regardless of the horrors I have faced turning away from them now seems like losing an old friend. There can be no denying that addiction was no real friend. Yet the dance I did with this devil became familiar and accepted.

In truth I had resigned myself long ago to the certainty that I would eventually die from a drug overdose or from a violent event. My biggest aspiration at the time was to die high. The life I led, as perilous as it was, was something I had grown used to and at times I now find myself, in dark moments, wondering if I am truly equipped to deal with this new life.

The difference between then and now is that of night and day. Now I yearn to grow, to make something of myself. If this transformation is not a miracle I do not know what is.

There can be no denying that I am better off now than I have ever been. I think hard and try to recall a time when I had these many options before me or this much hope for what the future holds and I come up empty.

Each day I must reaffirm my wishes to turn my will and my life over to God and each day as I lay my head down to sleep I realize that I have made it through another twenty four hours without using.

I have a new appreciation for life. I have hope and most surprisingly of all I have found empathy for my fellow man. It is no exaggeration that while I was in active addiction unless I thought I could get something from someone I wouldn't have given a second thought to other people difficulties, plights and troubles.

Soon I will be starting my training to become an addictions counselor and I know in my heart I am finally listening to my higher power and answering His call. I see before me a chance to benefit those I share this planet with, especially those who are still lost in their addiction.

By no means do I think that I can save the world but perhaps I can make a difference in one person's life. Maybe when I am presented the opportunity to give back I can save someone from the pain I endured and the pain I inflicted on those around me.

Recently I have had the chance to address local youth groups and I hope I have made a difference. I remember when I was that age and I thought I was indestructible; however I have learned now that drugs do not discriminate by age, gender or creed. Regardless of who you are they will seize upon the opportunity to drag you down, to rob you of your soul and to strip everything away from you. It is unfortunate, but for many that fall is six feet down and when they hit bottom they never get up again.

Each day brings new miracles, another day on the right side of the grass, the ability to start repairing the damaged relationships with those that love me, a new sense of self-worth and hope for the future.

Recently I celebrated one year clean. My family came to the celebration and I could see the joy and relief in their eyes. At the end of the day finding sobriety has been most beneficial to me; however there is great pride in knowing my family no longer has to worry if I am going to be killed in a bad drug deal, go to jail or die from an overdose.

Bruce flew out from the coast just to be here. How does one properly express the effect that friendship of that caliber has on you? How does one properly thank those that stood by you and helped you through the most difficult period in your life? Seeing these people there at that joyous occasion I was once again reminded of how blessed I am to have such a strong support group.

It breaks my heart to see those lost in their addiction not have the same.

Recently I have even had civil conversations with Susan and am now presented with a very real chance to have our son come out and visit me and my family for a few weeks. We have even had amicable discussion concerning finalizing our divorce.

Part of me longs for the chance to go back in time and take advantage of being married. I now realize that had we both worked on it we could have had something beautiful. In the lonely hours of the evening I still wish I had someone in that special type of relationship beside me to help me through the dark, to hold my hand as we walk through life.

I know that Susan's and my relationship will never be the same and in truth we are far better apart than we are together and I am learning to accept that and realize that it is for the best.

There were times in my past, when my heart was full of pain and cynicism, that I swore I would never get into another serious relationship. Now as I think on it I know I am not ready. I still don't know myself and learning to love me is still a work in progress; however I know now never to say never and I will leave that possibility in God's hands.

I am learning to accept life's ups and downs and I still am learning how to deal with emotions; yet now each day brings the promise of something new to learn. I no longer look at these situations as arduous but simply as part of the growing experience.

I spend a lot of my time still speaking to youth groups and visiting detoxification and rehabilitation centers. Although it pains me to see so many lost souls, I am buoyed by the prospect that some may find the same path to recovery and will live to experience the true joy of just being alive.

I am learning how to be real with people and because of that I have made a few new friends. Not associations based on using each other, but actual friendships based on respect and truly caring about each other.

One such person is James. Although I think we are totally different, we share a lot of the same pain from our past experiences with drugs and the associated lifestyle. Like me James is away from his children and obviously faces a lot of the same difficulties I do.

Through our shared experiences and our common desire to remain clean we have each found a fellow soldier in this war.

I have managed to maintain a relationship with a girl named Brook whom I met at rehab. Although in recovery, she has had more difficulties remaining clean. She has however proven to be a Godsend and someone I can totally relate to. Once again I have been blessed with her friendship and my support group continues to grow.

Our relationship has grown so strong that we refer to each other as brother and sister. As with my blood relatives I truly love her and want only the best for her life.

Recently I got the results from my latest blood test for Hepatitis C. I have once again been blessed by another miracle and have been told I can consider myself cured and that the disease only has a 1% chance of returning.

I recall when receiving previous test results that contained good news that the medications were working I would be filled with sadness that my desire to die was not going to be fulfilled.

I am still plagued by a fear of success. In reviewing what I have written, a cycle of obtaining success and then quickly sabotaging it is evident. I chalk this up to a lack of self-worth and so now as I reach new heights I worry that old behaviors will come to the forefront again and I will subconsciously wreck all that I have obtained.

I do think that now however I have been presented with the tools by which I can learn that I have worth.

In the past I have often heard people refer to experiences that helped them find themselves and most of the time I thought this was new age mumbo jumbo and had no merit. Yet I am truly learning who I am. I certainly wouldn't suggest a similar path for someone seeking an awareness of themselves yet I cannot disregard the fact that through this process I am learning all about what I truly consist of and what is important to me.

I started this book by saying that in no way was I going to be ignorant enough to say I had all the answers. As I grow older I find that more often than not I am uncertain as to whether I even want to know all the questions yet there are certain truths that I believe in now.

I believe, with all my heart that addiction is a disease, a disease that can be arrested and through hard work one can find a better way.

As with life there are no guarantees and so I will not lie and guarantee complete happiness in recovery. The road is often filled with potholes, ups and downs and setbacks, however I think that if one does do the work required and truly wants to quit using drugs it can be done.

For me the answer was within the twelve step group and the experiences of those that came before me and most importantly was found in my relationship with God.

For the addict that still suffers or the person in recovery my hope is that by delving into the depths of my disease as I have and laying my soul bare for all too see, they can learn that they're not alone. Past misdeeds can be overcome and we do not have to live in the shadow of guilt and shame so predominant in this potentially fatal disease.

To me addiction is a being that feeds itself on our guilt and shame. So often I was caught in the cyclical nature of the disease. I would be unable to handle emotions, be they good or bad, and so I would use drugs. I would then be filled with guilt and shame over the using or over the actions I took to procure the drugs and so once again being faced with these negative emotions I would use again and the cycle continued.

In recovery I have learned that I am not bound or defined by my previous actions and that even to one who has so many transgressions a new way is available. I believe now though that since I am aware that there is a better way I am totally responsible for the choice I make as to whether I choose recovery or the path of drug using.

I also hope that anyone who reads this who does not suffer from addiction may gain insight into the disease and how the mind of an addict works. So many of us are touched by this hideous disease and strength comes from knowledge.

For the most part I can now envision myself on that same beach I described for you at the beginning yet now I can believe that I have every right to revel in the beauty of that imagined day. I can believe that I was created with a purpose.

I pray that each and every person, regardless of their background, race, creed or religion also can feel the warmth, the sense of belonging and the knowledge that we are all here for a reason. We all have merit!

God bless.

"I don't ever want to feel like I did that day"

Under The Bridge
Red Hot Chili Peppers

EPILOGUE 1

February, 2009

I could not think of a better way to end the book then with input from a family member. What follows are the thoughts and feelings of my eldest brother on the night I received my one year cake.

For my brother and all in my family and my friends thank you all for the support you have given me through this trial, thank you for forgiving me for the damage I caused and know that I love you all very much. Sean

Hi, my name is Trevor and I'm Sean's brother.

Along with other members of Sean's family, I am here to support Sean and celebrate his first birthday.

As this is my first meeting it is an interesting and educational experience. It is exciting for me to put a group face to the organization and new friends who have helped Sean get to this birthday. I would like to thank you for your support and love for Sean and for each other as you try to assist yourselves and each other with ongoing recovery.

I think that tonight's reading was Step 11. "We sought through prayer and meditation to improve our conscious contact with God *as we understood Him*, praying only for knowledge of His will for us and the power to carry that out." As you took turns reading from the book and then sharing I was touched by your stories and by the level of care you have for each other.

As you were all speaking, things that you each said brought back memories of the last three years in Sean's life. I sort of feel like it is my birthday too since I have lived through part of his story and driven Sean to a few of these meetings over the last two years. Regular attendance did seem to coincide with improved effort and success.

Sean, I want to give you a hug and tell you how proud I am of you. As the people shared, my mind wandered and, I thought of the past two years, of the events a year ago and the false starts. I was thinking that if I stood up to speak that I would not be able to for the tears of joy and emotion. Tonight is probably the most emotional I have been about you since it all started.

As a family member I went through denial that my brother could be on drugs. I went through anger at what I perceived as your selfishness in pursuing this path. I felt disbelief when I contemplated the amount of money you spent and at the emotional cost for your son and your parents.

Every time you said that you were clean I tried to believe, till I stopped believing anything you said. Every time you sold something or asked for money my heart fell. I say these things now not to repay you with pain but as a counterpoint that makes my joy for you that much richer now.

I am sure that everyone here has had similar experiences to yours. I am sure that they have left behind friends and family in the pursuit of their addictions. I pray that they would all also have friends and family who stand behind them as they work on recovery and welcome them back as they attempt to live clean.

Anger and denial have kept at bay my feelings of hurt, pain, compassion and love. I think of the events in your addiction over the last three years and how close you came to giving up or being overcome. With this birthday I can begin to believe that you may have found relief, health and self-worth and I finally allow myself to feel FOR you, instead of trying to protect my emotions FROM you. I think that reading your personal assessment and poems on-line have helped me to understand your journey.

Tonight you celebrate one year clean. Not only have you stayed away from drugs for this period but now you also have a clean bill of health from your battle with Hepatitis C. One year ago I was reaching through an almost closed bathroom door trying to hold you while you thrashed around during an overdose. Your legs and arms were bleeding from cuts sustained flailing at the plastic shower stall, the toilet, the cupboards and the door. I was bleeding as well from cuts sustained from your nails digging into my skin and raking my arms. The police and the ambulance were on the way. What a contrast from blood and anguish to cake and joy.

In the past year you have progressed from:

- having your son removed to holding him and teaching him.
- being sent away by your parents to living again in their home
- living under the sentence of Hepatitis to normal life expectancy
- leaning on others to contemplating how to lift others up
- living for a fix to living for today

Thank you again to this 12 step group and once again…

HAPPY BIRTHDAY SEAN; I LOVE YOU!

EPILOGUE 2

May, 2017

Epilogue 1, written in early 2009, describes a happy ending to a long, painful and tortuous journey. However, any epilogue written before our journey is irrevocably over can only be described as the end of a chapter.

By 2016 the disease of addiction had again taken hold of Sean. In early 2017 he was still trying to "give back", still trying to help others off the treadmill as he counseled others in a rehab center while he fought his own demons. On May 3rd he used again but this time laced with Fentanyl! Thus the tragic story of an incredibly giving and talented man came to an all too early and abrupt end. Sean was forty-five years old.

As his brother Trevor wrote Epilogue 1 it is only fitting that he has the last word in Epilogue 2. R.P. Naish, Father.

Patrick Sean Naish: Eulogy
May 13, 2017

Today is a sad day.

Eight weeks ago I lost my wife to a vicious disease called cancer. Ten days ago we lost our brother, Patrick Sean Naish, to another disease; called addiction. It is easy to feel anger and frustration, to feel doubt and guilt. When someone goes too soon you can never be prepared. Even now I still feel both these losses sinking in.

Sean documented his personal journey and battle in his book; **"Through the Eyes of an Addict"**. In the last year he put it on Amazon along with a book of poetry. A number of you have read it and it has circulated by email in the last week.

My first draft at this eulogy was written too quickly. Facts but not heart. Today is a day to remember Sean's strengths, the way he made us smile and the way he reached out to help others. When I wrote Vickie's eulogy in March I started three days before her death by thinking about what I wanted to say to her before she left and that became her eulogy which I finished after her death, merging it with a letter she left behind for me.

I started Sean's too soon. It was clinical. I thought it was good but then as a couple of days passed I asked Kevin for some remembrances to thicken it and give it more of a true sense of Sean and a few things happened quickly that left me feeling Sean writing with me.

Kevin remembered the fun times we used to have golfing with Sean. The times spent joking and one upping each other with our takes on the Naish sense of humour. The time we drove though San Francisco and stopped at the side of the road and a four year old Sean ran back towards the Golden Gate Bridge to complain for his mom because it was orange instead of gold.

And then Kevin said he was going to wear an Oilers jersey to the service. Shirley posted on Facebook that everyone should wear an Oilers jersey today if they had one. And Edmonton scored 5 goals against Anaheim in the first period of game 6 going on to win 7-1 and tie the second round series. And I drove Elliott home in Sean's car and coming back I turned the radio up loud

And I resisted the urge to speed down Signal Hill towards Bow Trail

And I felt Sean beside me and I remembered our shared love of music, fun cars, hockey and being together

And I cried and drove past my house and drove around for a half hour before I updated the Eulogy and thought about Sean, who would rather be a wolf....

Sean at his best was strong, confident, joyful, loving. He enjoyed music, hockey and people. And he loved his son. And I miss Sean deeply for what he was and what he could have been

Sean had three strong passions. The Edmonton Oilers, helping others with addiction and, most importantly, his son Zachary.

Our family moved to Calgary in 1980 and, except for Sean, we all cheered for the Flames as they moved here almost the same time. For some inexplicable reason Sean cheered for the Oilers and had more jerseys, memorabilia and perhaps passion for his team than the rest of us Flames fans combined. And I was cheering for the Oil Wednesday night in game seven. Today he even got me to wear an Oilers jersey, though not without my Calgary Flames tie underneath.

Sean's struggles created in him a desire to help others who had the same disease of addiction. He wrote an autobiography, expanded his education and resume with counseling courses, and worked for many of Calgary's non-profit organizations working with the homeless, the addicted and youth. Despite, or because of, his own issues he made the extra effort to help those he knew with their problems. His late night conversations with Vickie as she dealt with cancer were a great source of support and he made a special effort to be there for her at home and when she was in the hospital. As Kevin told me last week "Just sitting around shooting the breeze and catching up, Sean had a natural ability to make you feel relaxed and at ease." The one on one times with Sean made you feel a real connection and that he was really centered on you."

Sean was 14 when he became an uncle and started out almost like an older brother to his nephews and niece as they shared in street hockey, birthday shopping trips, video games and TV. As Sean became an adult he tried to be there as an extra support as they went through their teenage years and transition to adults.

Despite the toll that addiction took on his life, career, marriage, and family, the one thing Sean was most excited about was being a dad and Zachary was the person whom Sean cared most about and was most proud of. Sean would make sure to take as much time off to be with Zach when he visited for holidays and summer vacation. Their time was often spent watching movies, playing X-Box, building Lego Star Wars kits, swimming, bowling, and their special meals at La

Vienna celebrating good school reports and time together; with Sean always making sure his regular waiter knew he wanted extra capers on his pasta. (I never understood the caper fascination.) Sean's book included this dedication to Zach "Mostly this book is dedicated to my son who, simply by being, saved my life and my soul. Zachary you are my inspiration and my hope for a better tomorrow."

I don't understand cancer. I understand addiction even less. I know there is no one to blame and maybe that makes it harder. I am trying to understand love and forgiveness. I am trying to understand God and his role in this world. It is my faith that makes me believe that my wife and Sean are in heaven, at peace and waiting for us.

Although relationships are strained and hard with addiction, Sean stayed close to his family. We will always remember good times and great memories of times shared with Sean. He almost never missed a special family dinner or birthday event. Not just family but numerous friends and co-workers all have memories of sharing coffee with Sean and discussing our lives as evidenced by Facebook posts, thank you and friendship cards that he kept and stories being shared this past week by those who shared his life. Sean enjoyed a good joke, sometimes some bad jokes, witty conversation and laughter. I remember some of the times spent together: mountain car rides to pick up Zachary for vacation, street hockey games, watching hockey, watching movies…

Today is a sad day for us. I pray that Sean is without physical and emotional pain. I pray that despite our sadness he can be happy…till we meet again.

POEMS FROM THE HEART OF AN ADDICT

By Sean Naish

Note: *I have never before felt the need to try and explain my writing. I haven't because of a few reasons. Firstly I assume that the reader is intelligent and can discern their own message from what they read. More importantly adding a prologue to a poem seems to me like trying to offer an itinerary for a dream.*

However the work I am presenting in this jumble of words carries with it a very negative tone and although I can truly say I am optimistic about the future knowing full well my worst day clean is better than my best day using, I am not immune to spending time in the dark recesses of my own creation.

The consequences of not ridding myself of these sometimes overwhelming emotions can be, with no exaggeration, terminal.

So please bear with me as I use you the loyal reader to attempt to rid myself of that which is foul. Too often self-doubt, shame and guilt seem to be the nourishment that the disease of addiction lives off of, hopefully in sharing that which is found below I continue to starve the disease.

PATRICK SEAN NAISH

A CONVERSATION WITH GOD

I enter your house feeling like a thief in the night
Enslaved by self-imposed chains, restricted by my own perceptions
Trying to hide from your sight I take my seat
I can smell hypocrisy and denial radiating from my pores
Real or imagined I cannot tell the difference
How humiliating it seems to so desperately need saving from myself
What double standard do I perceive to believe I am a sinner in a house of saints
Where do the thoughts of judgment and unworthiness originate from
Growing angry and resentful, pain leaks from my eyes.
Embarrassment, shame, self-imposed guilt
Who are you to offer me redemption
Do you not know me, what torture is this to tell me I am not terminally unique
The spotlight grows hotter, the fury builds
How else am I to express sadness, regret and loss but through anger
This is all I know, this has been all I wanted, this has been the source of my energy
Why give up that which has sustained me, how can one such as I be forgiven
Do not ask for me to be rational I am unaccustomed to it, these thoughts are all that I have ever given credence to
I have convinced myself I am alone, I have lived my life ensuring I would be
Now you offer to forgive, to accept, to welcome me back with no thought of my past
I am scared that I do not want to be forgiven, that I feel unworthy of that which you offer Conflicting forces battle within
In part I wish to surrender, in part I want to reject
Where do I find peace, a rescue from those memories that haunt my dreams

When do I receive serenity
How do I let lose my death grip on control
I am a prisoner in my own mind, you hold the key to my cell
I have but to accept it, to understand, to feel worthy of love
Help me in this, remove from me the self-deluded control that has led me astray
Since it was I who walked away will you truly be there to receive me
Help me to surrender
Help me to forgive myself

Patrick Sean Naish

A DAYDREAM

I stand alone behind all the other lemmings in the store
Waiting to play my part as a good little consumer
The wait continues and so I look around

To my left a young couple joke with each other
Their obvious loves radiates from them like a visible aura
Behind them parents play with their child as they to wait

I look down into my shopping cart and see frozen dinners canned meals
The food of the lonely

I close my eyes and daydream about the time when it was me in line with my family
My son looking up at me with unconditional love
My wife and I teasing each other about our purchases

A clearing of a voice brings me out of my fantasy
I have hindered the lady behind by slowing down her chance to throw her money away
With great trepidation I look once more at my cart
Still only the food of the single person is there
There is no child waiting to get home to play with his father
There is no wife waiting to snuggle on the couch

I long for what was, for what could have been, for what should have been
Regardless of this overwhelming sadness I smile
This is pain, just one of the many emotions I spent my life hiding from
I wore masks not to reveal my true self

I medicated so as to not have to feel
I understand that without pain there cannot be joy

Heading towards the door I cannot avoid one last glance towards the line up
Yet no magical transition has taken place
My family is not there

As I leave I realize I am faced with a choice
To dwell in this almost all consuming depression
Or to remember that I am lucky
Some have never even tasted the joy I received when this daydream was once real

I chose to be happy, to remember those times that make me joyful
To continue to dream and work towards the day when those smiles will return

Patrick Sean Naish

A HARD PATTERN TO BREAK

We hover above the user
Our presence unknown to him
We watch with sick fascination as the needle breaks the skin
The poison is injected

How could we not watch
This is a car accident, a train wreck
Ignoring the pending doom is impossible

Suddenly the user drops, it's been too much in the shot
Watch as the lightening courses through his body as he is tossed side to side
Gritting his teeth so hard shards of bone explode out of his mouth

The user is unaware of the horror of the moment, he will remember nothing
Those that love him and see the trial will never forget

Arms flailing, legs kicking, this small enclosure will be his down fall
Blood seeps undeterred from the gouges on his feet
The wood cuts into his hands without mercy

This is psychosis and it doesn't get much worse

Enemies from everywhere, people ready and willing to attack him
These are the images playing in the users head
He has no sense of reality
If he is lucky this will pass, if not this is his future
Forever stuck in this chemically induced torture house that only he can see

The episodes worsens, cursing an unseen foe, vowing death to everyone around him
He continues to thrash, to punch, to scream, to attack
Violence has never been so horrifying and yet so sad

Slowly the tremors lessen, the user eventually comes to
He has no remembrance of his actions
He wonders why his feet bleed so freely
Why his hands ring with pain

Understanding dawns on him, he knows he has had an overdose
The overdose has caused a seizure topped by a psychotic episode
The user knows he was close to death
Perhaps he has permanently damaged his brain

The user knows he is lucky to be alive and that the next one may very well kill him

The user is aware of the dangers
He is cognizant of the damage he has done to his body, his family his life
The User knows he must stop

The user steps out of the room and uses.

A NEW ROAD

Not so long ago I took a walk. As I walked I dreamt, as I dreamt I was visited by a guide.

The guide showed me a Sun brighter than that I had ever seen, fields of flowers in colors never imagined, streams of pure blue.

I saw beyond this peace a house, magnificent in design unparalleled in beauty

Upon my shoulder did the guides hand rest yet as I looked upon this vision his hand did tighten, as it did so did my heart. Joy departed my soul and was replaced by heartache.

I turned to my guide and a tear slipped down his face.
In the tear I saw the reflection of the road behind me overgrown with weeds
The souls of those I had wronged crowded together in a mist of sorrow created by misdeeds.

A different house sat before me, decrepit, haunted, and lonely

I gave in to the lament and found myself in the front yard of this newfound and yet familiar dwelling.

Desperately I look for the path to the place I had seen earlier, yet before me stood a wall.

Anger filled my heart and I lashed out at the barrier. I struck the brick of self-pity, turned and kicked the mortar of regret.

A hole opened before me, beyond the over worn path of fear I saw my guide a hand outstretched a hint of a smile upon his face.

I live still behind this wall, in this run down building but day-by-day I enlarge the hole and my guide waits for me still.

Patrick Sean Naish

A TIME FOR BLACK THOUGHTS

I close my eyes to sleep and the often repeated movie starts again
Too often I have seen the replay of those actions that haunt me
Can frustration and fear be any more perfected than this
Am I doomed forever to relive the mistakes the past

How sweet and bitter is this pain that refuses to leave me be
How incredibly vivid are the memories of those thing that make me shutter
I clench my teeth and attempt to envision happier times
My muscles taut I recall with trepidation the darkness of my past

I have painted those around me with the contempt I felt
I have covered them with the consequences of my disease
Too often I have played the victim, not realizing that I made victims of those that tried to help
How I long for a chance to let them know how my heartaches for what I have said and what I have done

Even now I hold this discomfort close like a security blanket
Repulsed by the shame and yet comforted by its familiarity
Apprehension reigns supreme as I contemplate the loss of those negative emotions I have become so accustom to
Too often I hide within myself reveling in that habitual need for negativity

Have I not already paid the Ferryman
Has the deal with the Devil not already been signed
Is it not to late to be cast out and forgotten
I cower from the despair that death will return at the end of a syringe

Is now the time I allow myself to cry
Am I allowed to shed tears for my own behavior
Will happier memories eventually replace the horror show I watch each night
Do I deserve the second chance I have been given

Where is the redemption I have been promised
Where are the greener pastures
Where is the brighter tomorrow
Where has the smile I carried for so long disappeared too

I long to rid myself of the black pit within my soul Is this emptiness self-created or a damnation of the disease
Can it be resolved, eradicated, annihilated
What will be left if all that is repugnant within me disappears

Patrick Sean Naish

AN ESCAPE FROM THE FLAMES

I stand before the flames naked
Head thrown back, arms outstretched
I do not fear the damage the heat promises
In fact I relish in the perceived pain

Consequences are tomorrow's concern
I step into the fire
Burn from my being the pain, remove from the memories
Melt my mind, my body my memories

I watch as the weight slips from my body, the morality from my soul
I become disfigured; a shadow of my former self as I languish in that that may destroy me
The flames have burned my eyes and I cannot see, the ash has filled my mouth and I cannot ask for help the heat has ruined my ears and I am def
I slip into oblivion

Too often I have awoken at the same door
Old with age an overuse, the name Death scribed across is blackened frame
How many times must I make the journey to this same place
How many before my could not resist entering the darkness that lies behind

Once again I am given reprieve
Yet again I have been spared
A tear rolls down my face and extinguishes the fire

Slowly I pick myself up, exhausted from the fight to survive

I tried for an eternity to bring death to the will I was given
If I still remain how can I argue a higher calling

I am surrounded now by those that love
No accusations slip past their eyes, no fault found in their looks
My charred hands leave the stink of my flesh on their clothes
There is no complaint only the desire to help

Now I lie in wait
My body, my mind my soul begin to heal
I will rise again

No longer will I visit deaths door
No longer will I hide in the flames
The next door handle I turn will lead me only forward

Patrick Sean Naish

ASSIMILATION

We float above and apart from your world
To us the conditions you live in are alien
We are the ones who have chosen a separate path

Occasionally we return to find those substances that keep us separate
Perhaps you have even seen us
The prostitute on the corner
The homeless man in the alley by the garbage
The Doctor who seems to miss more and more work
The business man who spends more time in the bar than with his family

Truly we do not know how to live in your domain
Your ways, your traditions are foreign

It seems your goals are family, career and happiness
We seem to revel in the loneliness of the broken hearted
Our aim is always the same, to spend as little time with you as possible
and to covet that which poisons us

Many in the past have tried to assimilate only to be met by ignorance and intolerance

Their fall from their flight never ended, no bottom could be found

Some returned only to lose themselves in the chains of self pity and denial that we often wear

When we do come back it is like learning how to walk again, how to talk, how to relate
For some our growth has been stunted for decades

The tradition into modern society is truly a slow and painful path
Those that chose to stay separate often whisper an invitation of return

Only through those that have managed to stay can success be found
Only through the relating of their trials and tribulations can we learn

There is hope for those that wish to reenter society; there is a path to follow

DREAMS REVISITED

Do you know what it is like to fear dreams
To lie awake at night until the darkness has lifted
The ghosts of your past whispering in your ear
How often are you visited by the memories of those things better forgotten

I know a place where Demons play
They lay in wait for my return
My eyes close and I drift to their domain

How many more nights must I listen to their chants
Visions of poison filled syringes
Glass pipes filled with pain Remembrances of unfilled potential
Crimes against my fellow man, crimes against myself

Shock

Horror

Tears

Regardless of the horrors found while asleep I know the sun will rise again
I will not succumb to the lies visited upon me in the night
My destiny is not derived from my past
I have new memories to make, new dreams await

Pride

Hope

Serenity

The bill has come due and I will pay it
Look for me at the finish line
Be with me as we create anew
I will chisel my existence from the challenges that lay before me

I am not limited by that which has past

Hold my hand and dream with me

PATRICK SEAN NAISH

ECHOES OF A CHILDS LAUGHTER

The times spent, his little hand in mine
We would walk the paths to the park
Previously unknown joy found in the relationship between Father and Son
The sound of his inquisitive voice, questioning everything would bring a smile to my face
Precocious in nature, innocent in his ignorance of life's harsh lessons yet to be learned
Satisfied in the knowledge of his protection and unconditional love

This is my Son, the embodiment of my hopes and dreams
No more perfect thing have I accomplished

The dream however was not meant to last
The knife has been cast and its target found in the centre of my back
The vision of the white picket fence gone

Harsh reality sets upon me; I can understand the undertow that led to this moment
Does he, can he?

I stand alone now on those very same paths we would walk
My hand the lesser for the lack of his held in my grasp
I hear only now the echoes of his laughter; I miss the look of happiness on his face

The swings stand empty, the teeter-totter unoccupied
It seems now only memories of ghosts exist
Should I not be bitter, should I not rage?

Does he understand why I do not tuck him in at night?
Why his Father is not there to dry the tears that forms after a scraped knee
Will he not look behind him while learning to ride a bike and not wonder where his Father Is?
What forces would deprive us both of these moments that are the things pleasant dreams are made of

I will forever wait upon these paths to the park if need be
I pray that one day I will look up to see his face as he runs towards me
The joy of our reuniting duplicated in his smile

Until than I wait
"Daddy loves you Zachary, Big time"

Patrick Sean Naish

FROM BLACK TO LIGHT

The disease is the color black
Obscuring all visions of a better way
Transforming itself from pigment into entity
It saturates itself through every fiber of my being
Like a cancer it spreads from finger to toe

It fills my soul with its foulness
Its filth distorts thought, its presence corrupts action
All must be sacrificed for its growth
It has become a foreign being within me that demands the ultimate sacrifice

I seem powerless to fight it and even more lost without it
Am I eternally bound to believe the lies it speaks
Forever more to be a slave to its demands

Rest easy and take a cleansing breath
There is a better way, a chance to shine light on the dark
To find a road where better things are waiting
Freedom, rebirth, love and hope are around the corner

Stand with me and claim victory in this first of many battles
We have been through all that is evil and corrupt while lost in our addiction
We have survived and is there not pride to be had within that
Each of us carry a piece to the puzzle, we have earned it through our trials

When we come together we can find an answer to the riddle
When we share and learn from each other we push back the black
When we listen to the pain of our brethren we find family

Miracles happen, joy can be found and love exists
These things and more dwell in the arms of those who came before us
Drink of the wisdom that is offered and share it with those who come after
Watch the rain fall each drop representative of a lost soul
Reach out your hand to one who is falling catch it before it lands
It may also be your salvation that exists within that single bead of water

GUILT

An old acquaintance came knocking
Traveled and worn
Strung out from his long journey

Somehow I must
Perhaps forgotten but not rid of
He reminded me that he had never left
I have been here through all that you have done

How could you have so easily forgotten
I came to remind you of your using
How you ignored your crying child in favor of the needle
The heartache
The crimes
The theft
The lies

Move on
I have come back to you now that you appear so
Weak and alone

Through me all is tainted
With me you can not move forward
I will hold you here with me, together we shall wallow

Be strong
Cry if you must I will not be cast aside
Have you not relied upon me
Was it not I who remained with you through it all

Help me God
Fear not I will come back
Remind you of your sins as often as possible
Together we can revel in your misdeeds
I will continue to feed your addiction
I know I can
Be
Free

Patrick Sean Naish

I'M SAD, I'M ANGRY

Alone in my basement am I not allowed to cry
To release the floodgates that holds years of tears
How does one describe a pain so deep, so consuming that everything else is secondary

Will I find a way to verbalize the torment I feel
Am I so alone in this discomfort that no one can understand me

There is truly a hunger for better things inside of me
Yet so often even the smallest roadblocks seem to refocus my attention to those things negative
I want to be happy, I deserve serenity

I have worked hard to be where I am today with no thoughts of retreat
However there still lies within my soul emptiness
There is no secret to the cause of this pain

My heart breaks each time I see a picture of his little face
I try and hold back the pain that slips from my eyes in the form of tears when I speak to him on the phone
I endeavor to make him realize how much his father loves him and misses him

Is it enough, does he understand or even at such an early age do thoughts of abandonment sit first and foremost in his mind
How can he comprehend the disappearance of one who so obviously loved him
I was given a great and beautiful gift in the life of my son, only now it seems to have been ripped away from me
I have struggled day to day to become the father this defenseless child requires and deserves

Yet I am trapped, locked in a cell of my own creation and all I can do is hope

Hope that one day soon we will be reunited, that I will be the role model he needs
Hope that through this all he is aware of his fathers love

I am told to "Be positive, look towards tomorrow, keep your eyes on the main goal and you shall achieve it"
Now as I sit here anger and sadness competing for my sole attention it all sounds like rhetoric

How can you not expect me to rage, not to lash out when it seems my anger is so completely justified.
There is not a day that goes by I do not work towards those things that will maintain my sobriety
Month upon month has passed and although I awake each day to have my heart break anew I seem no closer to being with him

I want to scream:
"You know nothing of pain"

There are those that appose my efforts to be with him and I serve warning to those people
This is my flesh and blood we discuss here
This is the embodiment of the greatest gift ever bestowed upon me

NOTHING
NO ONE

Will keep me away from him

Take heed; read my words carefully the battle that I would eagerly join to be victorious in that which is my right would be well beyond any you have witnessed before

Think not that I do not see my responsibility in the position I am in now
I have but to check my past to realize the part I played

However things have changed and I vow to bring the fight to you if you stand in the way of me and my son
Think of the child and his welfare, think of how it serves him, my son the most important of us, to be with his father.
Think of these things and put them into practice
Or think of the fight I will bring to your doorstep should you fail to think of my sons needs first.
Think carefully

I HAVE

I have seen the fires of hell
The flames leaving their marks on my arms
The scars trace their way up my veins

I have been in the company of Death
Too many times I have smelled the foul odor of the grave
The visions of my own demise forever scorched upon my memory
I have been witness to the depravity of the disease
I have seen those around me sell their soul for false hope and denial
Too often I have seen my Brothers and Sisters fall victim

I have walked the streets and slummed through the garbage
I have hidden from the light perpetuating my own dilemma
I have ran from the answer in fear of the unknown

I have confronted my Demons
I have faced my own insecurities
I have asked for help

I have been shown a better way
I have seen the possibility of a new beginning in the eyes of those around me
I have listened with tears in my eyes to the horror others have seen

I have been loved when I could not love myself
I have been lifted to my feet when I have fallen
I have been offered an outstretched hand

Patrick Sean Naish

I have gained hope, tasted cleaner air and felt the warmth of the Sun

I have work to do and the desire to accomplish it
I have a sense of freedom

I have tomorrow.

LIKE THE WOLF

To be like the Wolf
gathering strength and wisdom from those in the pack
to be better by those I surround myself with

To be like the bird
to rise above
to soar like never before

To be like the wind
Free and untamed
To be without restriction

To be like the clouds
To nourish others

To be aware
Aware that I am all this and more

To be without self-doubt
To know the truth of my potential

To know that through others I gain strength
To know that I can soar above my mistakes
To be free of the shackles that I place upon my person
To have potential, wisdom, courage
To realize these things are within my grasp or exist in me this day
To take pride in the knowledge that I am myself

Patrick Sean Naish

LOST MIRACLE

Slowly the daylight disappears, hidden in the oily slick cloak of night
Another chance of redemption seemingly lost am I always to repeat and never learn
Now is my time, my chance to crawl from gutter to gutter from crime to crime from high to new high
Another chance to finish my race to my six-foot deep bed.

I am lost, I am alone

Would I be wrong to sleep now
To cover myself in the sheets made of dirt
To consort with those that would eat my flesh
To perhaps lie awake for all eternity reflecting on the mistakes I have made

I am lost, I am alone

Emotion the enemy I have but one known weapon
I reach for the needle, I see in it only ecstasy, freedom from pain, reprieve
How is it that I am blind to the truth behind the deliverance of these false joys?
Behind the promise of enlightenment is the truth only shame, fear; guilt remorse lay within the devise

I am lost, I am alone

I have used all the weapons at my disposal to push back those who have loved me
Self-pity, isolation anger are my instruments of choice
I do not realize that these weapons are dull from over use, the blades rusted with the blood of self-inflicted wounds.

How do I not realize in my attempts to strike out it is I who also feel the cut of the daggers

I am lost, I am alone

I am anger personified, I am fury
My skin crawls over my bones like a river over the rocks
It is not just the poison that makes me clench my teeth in disgust
Have I asked for this lot, this damnation My soul screams can anyone hear me

I am lost, I am alone

Is it so dangerous, this self-realization?
I cover myself in the my over worn cloak of pity
Yet the smell of decay, of death from this garment sickens me
The weight of it no longer a comfort but rather simply a hindrance.

I am lost, I am alone

The hope and promise brought forth in a new day burns my eyes
Has this been delivered by those winged guardians from above Is it my Father who delivers me a moment of clarity
The fog cleared is it not a road that I see
Full of potholes, ditches, obstacles this path I know now at least holds the answer

Am I lost, Am I alone

I find myself in a doorway
I see before me souls much like my own, pain exists here but it is welcomed
Can I find the comfort I need in those that came before me

PATRICK SEAN NAISH

A hand outstretched offers no judgment, no condemnation only a smile of understanding
Tears try to free themselves from behind the mask of the day
With shaking hands, trembling body the taste of fear in my mouth I sit and I listen

I am home. Never again to be alone

MISCONCEPTIONS

The lawyer with a straw up his nose
The prostitute working to support her habit
The Doctor writing extra prescriptions for himself
The Mother substituting her morning coffee for vodka

The college student who overdoses on ecstasy
The cop who skims off the top of the evidence from a drug bust
The daughter who just tried heroin
The teenager who starts his day off with a joint
The man who hasn't slept since yesterday because of his taste for cocaine

The homeless man drinking mouthwash
The pro athlete who uses can't stop using his pain medication
The father who gambles his mortgage payments away

Do you see any difference?

Patrick Sean Naish

MY FRIEND

A tribute to you, my best friend
The only friend I have know
Having stood beside me through thick

You have reveled in my misery
Driven me to sink deeper
Held my hand as I was dying

We were never to talk, never to feel
Life was so easily devastating in your company
How often did you help with the transition to my end

Such a jealous friend
Attention only to you, not even I
Everything sacrificed for you

Hope, love
Family, trust, emotion
Self-worth
Gone to appease you

No more
No more No more
No more
Casting you aside
Realizing your attention was only to fulfill your own needs
How tainted, how sick

NO MORE

I WILL struggle through
No longer will I seek your approval
I know you for what you are

You will not hide your intention from me
I will not follow you down as you wish

When I fall do not offer assistance
I will crawl rather than be with you

I will find a new friend

Hope

Love

Emotion good and bad
I will walk with them now
You were with me through life
I CHOOSE that when I die it will not be within your company

Patrick Sean Naish

MY PROCESS

The process of acceptance and surrender so painful
I yearn for the rewards I envision
I wish for the something better wanting to be warmed by the sun of a new day
Yet I find inside of me a reluctance to work towards that goal

A desire to wallow in that which I have grown accustom
A fear of leaving behind the negativity that has sustained me
Realization that those emotions I have restricted myself to are destroying me

I beg to be forgiven and yet rail against that which I seek
I ask for understanding than complicate the process
I release my will and then question my faith

I am confused and desperate
Feeling a breaking of my will I rally my defenses
In part I so desperately wish to hide in the darkness
Truly I do understand that only through the light will I find life

I begin to understand I am worthy
I start to realize the goal is within my reach and it is only I that prevents it
Slowly and not without fight I begin the process of letting go

Opening myself to honesty and willingness I start to feel the warmth promised me
Confusion transitions into trust
Desperation seems to point towards serenity

I know that so long as I walk upon this earth the journey will never be completed
Yet I am secure in that realization, trying to trust in the outcome offered
Opening myself to emotions that are positive I continue

Understanding dawns with in me that being whole and feeling loved is all that has ever been wished for me
I struggle onwards expecting potholes in the road of recovery yet now with the knowledge of a guiding hand

I hope to grow accustom to the sensations of that love regardless of how hard I try and deny it.

Through this understanding, through honesty and through these difficulties I walk on evermore seeking the warmth of the Son.

Patrick Sean Naish

ONE LAST HIT

How did I reach this point
The consequences I so easily shrugged off earlier are back with vengeance
I should have slowed down
I should have rationed

A slow burning starts to build in my stomach
A dark pal slides over my mind
The black covers me head to toe
The spark becoming a consuming fire

I throw myself on the floor
My arms sweeping from side to side
Surely I must have dropped something
There can be nothing left

My chosen medication now only serves to build the panic
How will I survive with nothing remaining
How will I endure the pain that is to come

Fear gripes my soul
Nothing could get in the way of resolving the crises
No sense of morality left I would offer anything to gain more time in a haze

I thought nothing could exceed the hell of feeling
Yet here I am in the abyss of with drawl
My mind racing confusion sets in
Nothing is more important than ending this suffering

My thoughts drift to ending it
My muscles cramp with the realization of the horror
I have nothing to pawn, no money, no one to call
My heart races, sweat stains my clothing

I am desperation, I am fear I am sentenced to the anguish that follows
I cannot sleep, I cannot eat it is all consuming
I can hear the grinding of my teeth I can hear the whimper in my voice

Rescue me, deliver me from this torment
Provide me with one more dose

Can a picture of abject terror be painted
How can I properly describe a living nightmare
What words can I use to depict that which is unimaginable

My mind resolves itself to this visit with the devil
Waiting is the only cure for the suffering I must endure
Will I learn from my travels through the darkness
Will I avoid the poison that brought me to this point
Only the passage of time will reveal the secrets so vital to my survival

PURGATORY

It is no secret I can no longer hide the truth
I have walked through the fires of hell
Furthermore I have lingered in the place that would have eventually led to my demise

Countless times I have started to cross over
To go to the point of no return
I gave no second thought to the pain I would leave behind

Yet each and every time I was pulled back
Always I thought it a cruel joke
Brought back so that I could suffer further
So that I must endure more of that which caused me so much pain

Through the daily trials, the brushes with death I was unaware that I was moving forward
Guided by some unseen force, led towards at least an opportunity for better
Eventually I came to a door, a chance at redemption an escape from the torment

Entering this new room I was greeted by walls without substance
Grayness surrounded me, confusion ever present
It seemed like a holding place for the sins of all mankind
However there was relief here, a sense of a second chance
Before me sat what appeared an electric chair
Without knowledge of movement I found myself strapped in
A wet metal prod placed upon my head
My arms and feet tied to its well-worn wooden frame

Suddenly visions of past mistakes flashed before my eyes
I was forced to witness each and every time I lied, cheated or stole
All of the hurt I caused, the times I made the wrong choices
These things and so many more missed opportunities played out before me like some twisted movie

With each new scene I saw before me a jolt would flash through my body It felt like electricity, making my teeth grit
My arms and legs strain against their bindings

Through slow realization I came to understand it was not an electrical current
Each new shock consisted of shame, guilt, anger, denial and remorse
A direct correlation seem to lie between the action on the screen and the negative emotion I was subjected to

The more the pain and emptiness came to overwhelming me the more I seemed to hear voices from the door I had entered through

"There is no need for this" it would whisper to me
"You know I have all the substances and emotional repression you need to never have to face this again"
"Take from me this syringe, allow me to provide this chemical and you shall be free from your pain once more"

Yet by this point something had changed
An awakening had taken place
The voice no longer sounded soothing, no longer held the attraction it once did
Now I could recognize it for what it was, the embodiment of lies I focused on the door in front of me

From its bottom escaped a warm welcoming light
Full of potential, serenity and second chances

No longer was I restrained to the chair
My maturing had taken a positive step forward and now it seemed I was ready for the next stage
Still full of fear of the unknown I stepped up to the new door

I tried the handle to find that it was unlocked
Somehow knowing had I not endured what I did it would remain closed
Yet the doorknob turned easily in my hand

I opened the door to find a realm of unimaginable possibilities
The dishonesty I had grown accustom to was no longer required
The mask I had worn for so many years was not a prerequisite

This was the promised second chance
An opportunity at rebirth
I stepped forward

And………………………………..

REBIRTH

Like a new birth the sun breaks through the thick membrane of night
Casting aside the shadows that ruled for so long
Returning the world to a place of possibilities

For too long I dwelt in that darkness
Now as I see the tendrils of light work their way into the crevasses of my subconscious I know they are flushing out the Demons that took refuge there

Like new vegetation my soul grows toward the approaching light and rejoices in its return
How many times did I lose hope that there was a chance of victory
How many times did I resign myself to death

Yet now before me is the ultimate symbol of new horizons
New chances and untapped potential

Do you know of the hope I speak
Do you feel the same joy as I do in what can now be possible
Can you feel the winds of change and the secrets they hold

Forever I will see the dawn of each new day as a fresh beginning
Each time the sun rises it will signify survival
Whenever the warmth from the light brushes my face it will whisper encouragement to me
I have come too far, crossed to many obstacles, survived too many near death experiences
I am a bullet aimed directly at my target and although I know hindrances will arise
With the help of God I will see the target struck, the hope realized and the dreams come true

Think not that this solution is mine alone, I have visited rooms of kindred spirits that share the same outlook
As I do, they look upon themselves as survivors, survivors that must continue to learn how to live

When you have dwelt in the darkness, when you have forfeited everything for that momentary release of emotion what choice have you left than to try what has been proven to work

I know that the promise of the suns warmth is for all who require it
I have learned that we must seek it out and embrace the changes it brings

I have learned many things but most important to my soul I have learned hope

REPAYMENT

How much time did I spend on that road of decay
Trudging along the dirt filled path
Obstructed by boulders of denial

Downed power lines snaking across the ground charged with resentment

Fallen trees rotted from the inside by self-doubt

The skeleton hands of those who failed reach from the ground and drag me downward
I must be wary of the six foot deep potholes
The ghosts of my past whisper their lies and beg of me to turn back

The monkey grows stronger

I stand on my soapbox constructed from self-pity and proclaim to all the world

"No one has suffered as I, no one knows the extent of pain I have endure.
My slow suicide is justified"

Even as the words leave my lips I know them to be false, to be based on a need to be a victim
I see in the horizon a smoother path filled with people who walk with a purpose
They do not seem to limp from step to step, there backs straight the eyes fixed on tomorrow
They seem to have eluded the twisting, writhing deformity I have taken on in my illness

Still I see obstacles, I see hindrances to their path but no longer do the problems seem to be self-created they simply are and must be dealt with

As the dirt path becomes paved a sense of temporary elation fills my heart
To date I have survived and know that now I can prepare for the next day's battle
There stands a stranger at this cross road, a tear in his eye for my pain and a hand extended in love
We meet and he imparts his wisdom and the advice of those who came before me
I am told it is not my turn to venture forward; I must wait for the next to arrive
I turn my face into the hell I left behind and wait

Already a tear escapes my eye

Already my hand is extended

Time does not matter, I will wait forever if need be to repay the gift so graciously given

SHALL WE DREAM

Dream with me a dream about a dream
Transcend the world in which our bonds keep us grounded
Float above that which is restrictive to our freedom

We have danced with Death and now is the time to live
No longer can we allow that which is fatal to control us
We have but to seek out a better way and it can be found

Cast aside the chains of our slavery
Eliminate that which controls our destiny
There was nothing we would not do for the master of our confinement
Are we not willing to equal that effort to obtain our liberty

What is it that keeps you awake at night
What force controls your being so completely
What demons do you carry that are so absolute in their control

We have but to listen and to learn to cast aside our shackles
There are those who would provide the key
Can we not open our ears to their message

Are we so willing to forfeit, to bow down in the face of our common enemy
Stand tall and reclaim what you have been given
There is a war ongoing, to the victor goes your soul
Will we not learn of the tools that serve as weaponry in our battles

We stand at a crossroads we can visit the river Styx or we can persevere
What choice should we make; to resign ourselves to destruction or to come alive

Patrick Sean Naish

I have glimpsed that which waits for us, I have seen some of the promises
It is our right to claim that to which we are entitled

No longer do we have to be a prisoner to the poisons we embraced
Together and through each other lies the answer to the riddle
Each of us carries a responsibility to those who came before and those yet to arrive
We carry a duty to those who love us
We carry an obligation to ourselves

SOMETHING DEEPER

I have laid my soul bare for all to see
Without second thought I have exposed deep seeded fears
Delving into the pit of my being I have drudged up all that exists

Yet there is something deeper

I have plunged my hand into the slime of my past looking for my true essence
I have lain prostrate upon the table as the personal autopsy dug through my being
I have viewed myself under a microscope, examining all that I am
Yet there is something deeper
I have concentrated my observational powers on my essence
Too often I have lain awake analyzing all that crosses my mind
I have dived below the surface of conscious thought

Yet there is something deeper

What is it that leaves this whole in the centre of my being
What force, what persona has created this burning emptiness inside of me
Why is the core of who I am so elusive

How can I truly become one with what motivates me when I do not know who I am
How do I carry myself day to day not understanding who this person inside my skin truly is
Am I forever defined by my past

Can I truly exorcise those demons that plague my sleep

Answer me, relieve me of this burden

Who am I

Where are the answers to be found

If successful in my self-searching will I like what I find

Why does this personal journey scare me so
What lies do I accept as truth that bar my progress in self-realization

If I rid myself of all that is foul what will be left
Has not a lifetime of reveling in the darkness tainted my soul

Where is the key to unlock the mysteries I am plagued with

Why does someone not tell me who I am

How can what lies inside of me be such a mystery
There is truly something deeper
I do not know if it is through a lack of knowledge
Or an overwhelming fear that keeps me from gazing upon the truth of what lies beneath

STOP!

I see you walk away, your nose firmly fixed towards the sky
Do you think your callous nature goes unnoticed
What is it you fear
Do you shake with the thought you might see yourself reflected in his eyes

He is your Father, your Brother, your son
A victim of such a misunderstood disease
Would you be so cruel to one with cancer

Does he know there is a better way to live
Have you told him or is it easier to ignore the problem
How can you block his plight so easily from your mind

His hand is outstretched his soul in need of repair
However you have a bus to catch, a meeting to attend, surely someone else will help

How different are you from him in reality
How many times have you drank too much
How many times have you found it difficult to leave the poker table
How many times have you taken an extra painkiller

You should be bedfellows with shame
However you have chosen to spend your time with ignorance
Blind as you are, deaf as you can be you live in a world of black and white

If the roles were reversed would you not wish for the stranger to stop
To take the time to help
To have the desire to make a difference

Do not speak to me of things you care not to understand
Offer no solution that is based on indifference
You have yet to walk a mile in his shoes

What is the cost to you to offer compassion
Do you not understand it is your duty to help those less fortunate
I pray for you and your closed mind

How easy it must be to judge
To verbally spit on those you do not comprehend
Venom leaks from your attitude

Stop!
Open your eyes to the plight of those around you
Open your heart to empathy
Open your mind to the option of offering an extended hand

TAKE HEED ADDICTION

I hear you calling me
The dry dust from the grave exhaled with your every breath
I feel you constantly trying to invade my sobriety
For too long you have ruled my actions, my thoughts, my motives

For decades I have been a slave to your every command
I have dedicated myself to those attributes you hold in such high regard

Self-pity

Denial

Manipulation

Has there ever been a time when I did not see you an unstoppable force
How long did I feel that I could never defeat you
Many years wasted when the truth was I had no desire escaping your grasp

For so long I envisioned that you had been sent to destroy me
To use me as a tool to not only to create havoc in my life but also in those that loved me
Your sole intention to take control of my life, my mind my soul

You seemed destined to control all that I am and all that I would ever be
However I am learning to see through you and cast you aside
Through self-realization I have seen the truth of where you gather your strength
I have peered through the façade that you used to blind me these many years

Patrick Sean Naish

I know now your strength comes from me

Return to the depths of pain where were you came
Hide yourself from my newfound understanding
We are at war you and I, my hatred for you will burn forever more
Day by day I learn the tools to keep you at bay

No longer will I heed your call
No longer will I do your bidding, a bidding that only ever led to my self-destruction

I know that I carry strength, a connection with God
Your attempts to blind me to this strength have become weakened
With this knew found empowerment and the force I gather from those that love and support me I will be victorious

I cast you out and take back the power I have given you
I remove the blindfold you used to shield me from the truth
I open my ears so I can hear your lies and know them for what they are
Do not think this will be the end of it
I have seen how you use people
I have witnessed how you encourage them to lie, to cheat to steal

I am cognizant of your tricks and I will use this knowledge against you

With this knew found knowledge I will endeavor to teach, lead or simply be the one beside those who still you.
I know you and I know the evil you stand for

Yet I also know your weaknesses

Truth

Self-Realization

Empowerment

I will use these weapons to help others overcome your grasp on them
Take this as a warning you were unable to kill me regardless of your many attempts
So from now on I will be there as often as I can to thwart you

Patrick Sean Naish

THANK YOU

For the difficulties
For all the pain
The Strife

Thank you

For all the doubt
The loneliness
The Fear

Thank you

Because you held my hand through it all
Because of the lessons learned
Because you never left me
Thank you
When I stopped listening you continued to speak
When I perceived loneliness you were there
When I walked away you waited patiently

Thank you

Through strife I learned success
Through despair I found love
Through pain I learned joy

Thank you

Without you I would not know comfort
Without you I would be no more
Without you I would be less

Thank you

You held me when I cried, listened when I screamed
As you have been before you are with me today
Waited as I found the path

Thank you

For the knowledge you will be with me always
For the blessings and miracles delivered
For honoring the promises given

Thank you

For acceptance
For hope
For trust
For love

Thank you

Patrick Sean Naish

THE HUNT

The routine is started again
The hunt is on, the call has been made
Already the adrenalin courses through my body
The anticipation burns out of control through my thoughts

I have but forty five minutes until I can once again taste my misguided perception of Heaven
How can I possibly wait out this insurmountable amount of time
What could possibly divert my thoughts for so long

I decide to head to the pre-approved meeting area just in case he is early

They never are

I fiddle with the radio but my interest lies in the poison on route
I try and let my mind wander to thoughts not related to the escape I foresee

Every car that enters in the parking lot makes my heart race
Every person I see for a split second looks like the one I am waiting for
I feel I am about to burst

Even now I can taste the smoke that is soon to fill my lungs
I can feel the death traveling up my veins to my brain

A recognizable vehicle enters, it is him
I try and control my excitement but I am shaking with anticipation
My stomach does cartwheels as I realize how close I am to forgetting all that troubles me

The deal is done, the provider of deaths assistant has left
Do I seek a safe place to start the journey
Do I worry about who might see me
No

Without second thought I stuff the pipe
Without regard I break the skin
Without worry for any problems it may create I take flight

What was it that only yesterday was breaking my heart
I don't seem to remember anymore

Was it not just hours ago I felt the guilt of hurting those around me
I don't seem to care anymore

Was is not just a short time ago I worried about the trouble this lifestyle brings
I don't seem to harbor those same concerns anymore

I am flying, I am free from all that has bothered me
I am fixated on chasing the dragon
I am no longer myself, whoever that may be

Tomorrow the cycle will begin anew
However consequences are other people's concerns

Later someone will find out and will weep for me
However consequences are other people's concerns

My soul will be damaged by my actions this day
However consequences are other people's concerns

Patrick Sean Naish

One day this will land me in a grave or in jail
However consequences are other people's concerns

I am an addict
So therefore consequences are other people's concerns

Or are they

I have forfeited my families trust for this pursuit
I have given up my own sense of morality and dignity for this desire
I have thrown away all that I once held dear for something that is killing me
Perhaps consequences are truly my concern

THE JUDGMENT

The judge sits in his seat of infallibility obscured by a mask of unreason
Ready to cast down upon me the punishment for my sins
Contempt radiates from behind an aura of supremacy

I plead guilty to all that I have been charged with
I seek no mercy for the acts I have been found guilty of and those I keep hidden
I implore the judge to consider my efforts to fix my life
My attempts to be respectful, honest and clean

A booming voice casts my defenses down into the gutter
"You are beyond forgiveness"
"Your violations have caused pain for all of those around you"
"You have neglected the gift of life so freely given to you"

I am devastated, beyond redemption, without salvation
If the judge is to be believed there is no hope
No better life
No answers
No reprieve

Those around me come to my defense, even those I hurt most deeply
"Your Honor" they say "We have found it in our hearts to forgive, why is it that you cannot"
The love of their actions, their ability to move on brings warmth to my heart

"It is not my fault that you are all blind" the judge replies
"He has gone against all that we stand for"
"I find him guilty"

"His punishment shall be shame, guilt, remorse, heart ache"
"I shall never allow him to be free of the emotional consequences of his actions"
The verdict has been cast; his job done the judge prepares to leave the court

Slowly the mask he hides behind, that which gave him his power fades

I see the judge for what he is, I see the man who refuses to forgive me

I see he who would have me forever feel the weight of those past misdeeds

I look closely in his eyes and see myself.

TOGETHER

Unabated they flow through me like a torrent
There used to be a medically created damn to slow their progress
Now there is nothing between me and the emotions that I have kept locked away for all of these years

Please tell me how I can describe the essence of a tear, is there a story to be told in each drop
How does one suddenly learn to accept joy when it has always been such a misunderstood feeling
Does the rage I hold have justification

I have lived my life carrying chains that few can see
I have struggled under their weight and crawled due to their encumbrance
Why did it take me so long to learn that the key would have been so freely given

All I had to do was ask
All I had to do was overcome my self-imposed limitations and false beliefs
I now realize I am stronger because I was able to mutter those four letters
I now know I am alive because I swallowed my fear and cried out

Do not judge me or my kin
We are not adept at living in your world
We have had years of practice standing apart
Medicating ourselves with whatever substance could be found

Yet here we are trying to learn to walk, some stumble, most regrettably never get up again

We lived our lives desperate for someone to lend aid
Yet terrified that we made be heard

Can you understand the double standard of wanting salvation and yet being in total fear of what that salvation may represent

Does it not make you stop and wonder what emotions we deal with when we realize that we tried slow suicide and to some of us it only showed us something else we had failed at

We gather in rooms full of overly repeated stories, rehashed problems and stale coffee and yet in this group we find empathy, direction and love.

Together we try and learn how to integrate into a world that for so many years has seem completely foreign to us.

Together we learn to overcome our daily struggles

Together we learn to live.

Together we can

TWO DIRECTIONS

I stand on the crest of a hilltop
Stuck between two worlds, two destinies
From in front of me a warm, comforting wind gently brushes my skin
From behind a bitter, foul smelling gust pierces through my clothing

The crest becomes a tightrope that I must balance on as I choose my path
Swaying back and forth, assaulted from behind and comforted from in front
I look down to the valley floor and see only hope and possibility
It is as if tranquility has found a home, beauty resides in this direction

Across the horizon a myriad of colors seem almost painted across the sky
The vision so awe inspiring it catches my breath and brings a tear to my eye

I know what lies behind me; there is no need to look
This is the direction from where I came
It is a desolate place full of despair and regret

The half-dead trees seem to reach out at you with branches that resemble skeleton hands
The path itself is infested with weeds that cover everything like a virus
A sky so dark, so bleak truly only the blight of the grave could be worse

I traveled this realm of lost hope for more than half my life
At times I gave myself over to it, deciding to reside their until my eventual demise
Through God and with the help of those who love me I was able to escape to where I stand now

Yet even knowing what I do of that which lies behind me I find it difficult to move forward
For so long I was entrenched in a daily battle just to survive
I had long given up on the dreams of the everyday man
My goals began and ended with the piercing of a syringe in my skin

What is it that makes me hesitate, why is it I have not already begun the journey to the valley floor The once present yelling from my cravings have become whispers
I no longer see an attraction to the lifestyle
Truly my wants and desires have changed it is no longer enough just to survive
Now I wish to live

However on this tightrope I stand
Wondering why I do not move forward
Then like a revelation it dawns on me, before me lies the potential of fulfillment
A sensation I am unfamiliar with

It is possible to fear success
One can become so used to sorrow that it seem the norm
We can be conditioned to expect the very least of ourselves and somehow think we are satisfied

I know now that the path behind me leads only to my demise
It is only the path in front of me that I must concentrate on
Putting aside my fear, dealing with my anxiety I step forward

I am deserving of what lies below
Too long did I imprison myself in the hell I came from
It is well past the time that I took what is attainable

Hope
Prosperity
Serenity
Love
Trust

These things and so much more await my homecoming
And so the next leg of my journey begins…………..

Patrick Sean Naish

WHO AM I?

Do you not know who I am
I am your confidant, your friend, your advisor
I am the one who be with you always

Forever more to be that voice in your head
The compulsion you feel, The burning unquenchable desire
Trust in me, I will not leave you

Descend with me into the darkness
Our journey is but six feet down
I have all that we will need on the way

I have liquefied death
powdered poison
capsulized depression

Do you not recognize me yet,

I am all…..everywhere and everything
I am the blood on the knife
I am the crying abandoned child
I am the bullet wound in the cashiers chest

I am the end of your family
The destruction of your self will
The curse upon your morality

You can never walk away from me
I am more unto myself than you will ever be
Many have tried to leave me, many stronger than you and I have sharpened my teeth on the bones of them all

Lay at my feet all that you have earned
Give unto me your self-respect
Empty your pockets, sell your possessions
Your debt to me is never filled

How is it that I am still unknown to you

I have enslaved generations, prostituted entire Countries
I am an epidemic upon this land I am a plague for which there is no cure

Look into my eyes
Does it frighten you to see your own reflection so cleverly distorted
You look upon yourself, yet where there is courage I show cowardice
Where there is strength I show weakness
Where there is hope I show isolation

Crave for me, Lust for me Seek me out
Forsake everything and everyone to answer my call
What wicked joy I feel when you find me and I know I will only make you start the cycle again

I cannot still be unknown
Look closely
I am death, I am the fires of hell
I am the entity that squeezes your soul between my oily hands
I am your addiction.

Patrick Sean Naish

YESTERDAY AND TODAY

Scars on my arms
Scars in my heart

Tears in my soul
Horrors in my head

Constant reminders of a yesterday
The weight of which threaten to carry me under

A longing to plunge six feet down
The need to turn from the sun

The price was high
Never did I question

Life sacrificed for the needle
Poison replaces will

Healing at hand I turn to you
A better way is promised

New understanding unfolds
A fresh path is revealed

My bill has come due
Together it can be paid in full

I do not fear tomorrow
I yearn for the miracles offered

No longer afraid of yesterday's shadow
We walk together
Together
Forever
Into the Future

Give me relief
Open my eyes
Deliver me

ABOUT THE AUTHOR

For the better part of 23 years, I had the honour of calling Patrick Sean Naish one of my best friends. To say that Sean had a unique sense of humour is an understatement. Sean loved to laugh. He mastered the art of sarcasm like no one I had ever met. But as many people knew, or learned very quickly, this was just one side of Sean. Sean was a proud father, and a loyal friend. His son Zachery was the most important thing in his life. He loved and cared for his family, although he would be the first to admit that he tested their patience on several occasions. The phrase "I've got your back" is used very frequently in today's society. When Sean said it…..he meant it. Sean would often go out of his way to offer a sympathetic ear, a shoulder to cry on, putting others ahead of himself so their battles were a little less of a challenge. I've always known how much Sean meant to those he was close to…. but what I recently learned was just how many lives he truly touched. Through his work as an addictions councillor, Sean helped many chart new paths to overcome their battles with addiction. Sadly, the battle that was toughest to overcome….was his own. Sean lost that battle in May of 2017. His legacy lives not only through his son, but through the pages of this book. "Through the Eyes of an Addict" is Sean's story.

Ray Beattie

www.ingramcontent.com/pod-product-compliance
Lightning Source LLC
LaVergne TN
LVHW091533070526
838199LV00001B/41